Steel Meadow Farm

Stephen Craig Mathis, Author

Independently Published
Kindle/Amazon

ISBN: 9781693915918

Copyright 2019

All Rights Reserved

Stephen Craig Mathis, Author

Schedule Steve Mathis to speak, sign books, or give his testimony. Please contact: SCMathis2003@Yahoo.com

HoltPublishing.Yolasite.com
HoltPublishing4U@Gmail.com

Business Website:
http://vikingsteelinc.com/scrap.html

Credit for author photos: Casey Mathis
https://caseymathis.smugmug.com/Steel-Meadow-Farm-Book-Pics/n-KW6cn9/

Special thanks to Conner Mathis for the artwork on the cover, and Alex for typing.

Note from the Author:
Although this is a true story, names of the wicked have been changed to protect their identity, give them no place in this book, and to avoid potential frivolous legal challenges.

TABLE OF CONTENTS

5	Introduction
7	Dedication
8	Quote from the Author
10	The Beginning
14	Moving to the Farm
17	The New House
20	The Undoing
28	Hunting Journal
36	Going Back, Walking through Hell
38	The Hospital
41	The Funeral
43	The Aftermath
46	The Apostasy
53	Tribute
54	July 2010
58	The Exodus
60	A Promise
64	"Plow it under."
66	The Rebirth
69	Every Boy's Dream
72	Diamond in the Moonlight
73	Back to the Missionaries
76	Day of Preparation
77	SWS
79	Rufus Whelchel
81	Working at GE
85	Teaching at Sptbg Tech College
86	TEC
88	Collision with Fate
98	Godfather Number Two
101	Joe Garrett and Jesse Black
103	The New Fabrication Shop
106	Bankruptcy, Trial by Fire
115	SWS - June 29, 2012
118	Textile Town, Textile Ruin
122	Dean Bemel with Limco
124	George Gillespie
126	Kerkle Enterprises - SCDOT
127	CDL
128	Wigington Scrap Metal
133	Farm Lake
134	Stephen Cross Mathis
136	Juan
139	Homecoming
143	Ed Brigman
144	Isaiah 54
148	Breaking Forth
149	Annabelle
150	Battle over the Land
152	Stop Here!
155	Day of Détente
157	Health-Tex
163	Billy Tobias
166	Sticker Shock
169	Brad Cogdell
173	July 24, 2015
175	RJ and Joey
179	Ken Bolin
181	K-Mart
185	Kohler
187	Spool Cleaning
189	American Fast Print
195	Storms, Tempests, Broken Deals, and Death
196	Grandmother Mathis
198	The Collapse
200	Potter's Store
202	Martin Drug Store
203	A Gold Pocket Watch
205	Thanksgiving
207	December 14th
212	Christmas Eve
213	My Gethsemane
214	Breach of Trust
217	Easter Bunny
219	Jim Rivers
221	Viva la Mexico
224	Mystery Solved
228	Yo-Yo's and Promises
230	A Ride to Charlotte
235	Will you be Faithful?
238	My Broken Heart
244	The Gun
252	Deliverance
254	Steel Meadow Farm
259	Leave a Legacy

Bridge, Grandma & Grandpa Mathis, Steel Meadow Farm House Plans, Demolition Job

STC Plans, Downtown Clock Tower, Goldie, Imploded Andrews Bldg.- See Cross

Introduction

The story of *Steel Meadow Farm* is a story about my life growing up in a small town called Cowpens, South Carolina. Throughout the 12 years it took me to write this book, I revisit the vast memories of growing up on a family farm, my conversion and membership into The Church of Jesus Christ of Latter-Day Saints, and the tragedy and triumph of Steel Meadow Farm.

Growing up on a farm was wild and exciting for me and my brothers. We loved the freedom being able to roam free gave to us. This story depicts traveling sister missionaries who converted me to the gospel as soon as I heard the story of Joseph Smith, and *The First Vision*.

It depicts how a farm that had been in my family for 4 generations, and a new house that my father had just built, could suddenly be taken away by tragedy.

Stephen Terry Mathis

American Angus Association

Stillmeadow Farm

August 27, 1968

This book takes the reader on a 30-year journey. From the day an 18-year-old boy had to bury his dad, watch the family farm being sold, and makes a promise to his two younger brothers: "Someday, somehow, it's gonna be ours again!" All my life has been about work. I was determined to not let the tragic death of my father be the end of my family. Over the years, I worked very hard, and very long, retracing the steps my father made to become a successful business man. After all that I could do, it was my faith, and knowledge, that my Father In Heaven was by my side and blessing me from above, that carried me through each day. After making that promise to my younger brothers all those 20 years ago, I could have never expected, or imagined that all my life God was working His perfect plan. The book explains how Heavenly Father qualified me through faith and hard work to see His miraculous gift given back to me, my return back home, back to the *Steel Meadow Farm*.

Romans 5:3-5 *"And not only so, but we glory in tribulations also: knowing that tribulation worketh patience; and patience, experience; and experience, hope: And hope maketh not ashamed; because of the love of God is shed abroad in our hearts by the Holy Ghost who is given unto us."*

Steel Meadow Farm - October 29, 2003

Great men in the past have at times been commanded to write. Isaiah, Nephi, Peter, James, John, Paul, and all the other great people in biblical times felt as though their experiences in this life were worth tremendous value to the human family. The reasons that compelled me to write this book will be manifest and will be primarily for my posterity and all others who will read this work. It will be to the humble acknowledgment that Jesus Christ lives! This amazing story of my family and life will illustrate that many miracles can and do take place for the faithful and obedient children of our Father in Heaven.

Dedication

To my wonderful wife, Angela, it is because of your faith and love for me that I have been able to accomplish so much. Your love has been the wind beneath my wings, and the beat of my very heart.

Angela and Stephen Craig Mathis

Quote from the Author

"It is not often that love and fate seem to outline one's path to happiness or sadness. I am a firm believer in man's free agency to choose his or her own way. However, it is still amazing to me that in my life it seems as if unseen forces, or fate, keep determining my destiny. I have come to realize that as I put my faith in the Lord, many miracles have, and do continue to occur. This book will be a recollection of the events of my family and my life. The events that brought me from a life of obscurity and poverty, to owning successful corporations, being a father to a wonderful family, and back, yes delivered back, to the Steel Meadow Farm. There are times when love is very powerful, when prayers are heard, when faith is rewarded with blessings, and miracles fill our eyes with tears. At these times, we realize how much we are cared for by the unseen and blessed with the tender mercies of God."

4/28/22

Sydney,

"MAy God Bless you always"

Stephen Craig Mathis, Author

The Beginning

My earliest childhood memory came as I struggled to get past the wooden bars of my crib. The small blue and white trailer that we lived in seemed very large and spacious to a three-year-old boy. I remember how beautiful my mother was. Her name was Mary Ann, and she had long black hair. She was always the most pleasant person to be around. She was charming, flirtatious, and seemed to know everybody in our small town.

Mary Ann Moore Mathis

Memories of my father in those years were very vague. He was always working. I can still remember how much joy filled my heart when he came home. I remember the sound his welding truck engine made as it pulled into our driveway. I recall the smell of cowhide leather, denim, and welding smoke from his welding shop. He always seemed to me to be the happiest of all people. He was a very stocky man with blond hair, blue eyes, and a huge smile.

Steve and Ann Mathis on their Wedding Day, January 18, 1964

Dad and Mom at work.

Good Mentor

Dad sitting high on the steel – look to the left.

Ann (Mom) and Steve (Dad) in the office.

He seemed never to meet a stranger. Lots of folks came around to borrow money with a promise to return. I can truthfully say that I never heard him turn anybody down. He was always doing something for somebody who was down on their luck. And though I didn't know it at the time, he had been very experienced in hardships, disappointments, and trials as a child and young man. I never knew that my dad, the most confident, self-sufficient man I ever knew could be depressed and insecure about himself and life. It would only be 15 years later that the magnitude of this would be felt.

We lived in the blue and white trailer for a while, and I had a baby brother named Clint. It sure was nice to have someone to play with. Not long after that, we moved into a brick house in a development called Ivy Park. Three years later the third baby boy was born. His name was Clay and he seemed to make our family complete.

After all, having two brothers was better than having just one, I thought. For 10 years or more we were the closest of brothers, no one messed with the Mathis brothers. Fight one and you fight them all! This was the law that was given to us by my father. It was the basic knowledge of all our childhood associates that the

Mathis boys stuck together, no matter what. We knew and understood as children the Holy importance of family. How could we be prepared, to one day, forget this fact? Impossible?

Our Old Home

Ann, enjoying the front porch swing.

Farm House

Moving to the Farm

The day came when we moved from our rural development to the family farmland. It seemed that my father purchased a four bedroom farmhouse from one of my grandpa's sisters. The house and 5 acres backed up to my Grandpa Mathis's 54 acre cow farm. It was the case that he had bought it from his mother for $74 an acre. The following story will explain how the land value would increase 70 times in the course of my life!

The farm! I was truly amazed at the remarkable lay of the land. It had a combination of timber, hardwood, and rolling pasture. My grandpa nurtured the land like a mother over a newborn. He was very particular about everything. He could detect how much damage his three grandchildren could do to his farm. He could tell if we had been in the corn. He could tell if we chased the cows. He knew if we had been in the barn. He knew if we had crossed the fence just by looking at the barbed wire. But as the laws of nature took place, we learned to avoid him like the plague, and we took our liberty to run the fields and woods with all the joy and freedom of our little hearts and imagination.

It is very difficult to describe just how addicting the smell of fresh cow manure and fescue grass can be to a young boy. There are times that it can bring the most relaxing feeling to one's mind and soul. I remember the sound of barbed wire fencing creaking as you climb across, the ripple of the water in the creek, the wind blowing through the pines, and the tall Kentucky fescue grass, the lowing of the cattle and the sound of mama calling us home. These are the sounds ringing in my memory and etched in my mind and in my heart. It was the most beautiful place on earth to me. The land can be harsh. Wild roses that refuse to relinquish their hold on the land would tear your clothes off your body. The poison oak, Yellow jackets, hornets, and Copperhead snakes made you constantly aware that there is a price to pay for all the joy encountered on the farm.

From the top of the hill of our old home we could see the Blue Ridge Mountains and the beauty of ours and my grandpa's land. The sun would rise to our front porch and set in the evening on our back porch. Those golden sunsets, picturesque snowcapped mountains, the pines, and the beautiful meadow created a love affair within my soul for this piece of land. It was something I cherished as a child, a deep affection, and a love affair, that never left me as a man.

After we moved to the farm, my dad's welding business, Steve's Welding Service (SWS), began to grow out of control, and so did the three Mathis boys. We were goodhearted, but absolutely wild as bucks. We threw rocks, apples, potatoes, and anything else in season at each other, as well as any occasional passing truck or car. Any vehicle that appeared to be traveling toward our little glorious town of Cowpens, South Carolina, suddenly became a target. The excitement and terror of hitting a moving vehicle with a snowball or tomato was absolutely, glorious, to us boys growing up on the farm! From the thud, to the screeching brakes of the vehicle, we would run fast as we could, and hide in the woods. It was like playing Army.

Goldie

All of us boys excelled in sports. We loved motorcycles, our pony horses, and both were driven hard and fast. It is no wonder our horses ran from us. We only knew one speed and that was wide open! As time went by, Clay and Clint began to fight with each other a lot. It worried me because as my daddy put it, "I was my brother's keeper". He would whip me just because my brothers fought. He would say I was in charge, and I was letting them fight. I never could understand why they began to resent each other so very much. Looking back now, I can see that Clint grew up caught in the middle. After all, he was the middle child. I was the big brother in charge, "the keeper." Our little brother Clay, the baby, was spoiled rotten and learned at an early age to manipulate my parents. He would pit them against each other to get his way. If mother said no, then daddy said yes. Who could have guessed just how debilitating that would be in both of my brother's lives? Time would only tell how great the consequences would be.

The New House

After a few more years on the farm, a stir of excitement was being generated between my father and my mother. We boys soon heard the news that Dad was going to build us a new house! We didn't think too much about it at the time. There were apple trees, grapevines, and scuppernongs to reap the rewards of. But soon, the bulldozers, backhoes and other earthmoving equipment began to catch our attention. It became a reality that we really were going to build a new house. The house would have a basement. This sounded really cool!

I can still remember the sound of the hammers ringing as the house began to take shape. When it finally emerged, I knew what all the excitement was about. It was a mansion! Nothing of this nature had ever been built in Cowpens. It was amazing! The new house would be a traditional Southern brick colonial style mansion house, with four big white columns, and a winding staircase. It was somewhere in the 6000 square feet range. The masonry was called Antique New Old Brick. It looked so unbelievable, and the sad irony was that it would be, in fact, unbelievable to me for the next 30 years.

Within, and here, in these next lines I will attempt to convey all the heartbreak and sadness that was on the horizon for our family. And even though this story and events seem incredible, it is by my hand that I certify the truthfulness of my recollection of the following events of the Steel Meadow Farm. Memories I can still, in my mind, feel. The hot summer breeze and the smell of the tall fescue grass as I stood in the field with my dad overlooking our land. The day I first heard the term "Steel Meadow Farm." It was the name that my father had chosen for the farm, and I can still to this day hear him say, "When I buy the rest of this place from grandpa, son, I'll call it "Steel Meadow Farm." I have wanted to call it this name ever since I was your age. And because I have a welding and steel erecting business, we will spell it Steel, instead of Still. I approved and agreed as energetically as a 13-year-old boy could. He also said that he was going to buy a registered Angus bull to start a herd. He said we would name the bull the "Iron Butterfly". This sounded great and was music to my ears. He talked of building a pond in the bottoms beneath the spring. He said it would be a beautiful pond. He showed my mother and us boys the survey flags and pins that the Army Corps of Engineers had placed to outline the perimeter of the pond. The idea of swimming and fishing in our own pond was very exciting to us three us three boys. I could hardly wait!

Pond as it is today.

The wait for me to see the pond would be over 20 years. The pond, the land, the Iron Butterfly, and herd, would be something not to be for my dad in this life. This is the real tragedy of the Steel Meadow Farm. For even as I love the farm, there was one who loved it like no other. A person who already saw it for what it could be. One who could see and feel what others could not. This land belonged to his earthly father, but this land was a gift from his Heavenly Father. My dad knew and appreciated this sacred fact. The place was his refuge, his solace, a place to hide, a place to ponder, a place to pray. Many times, I saw him kneeling in the woods by the stream in fervent prayer. Many times, I saw him stroll across the hills he would never possess, dreaming of the day he would, and of the day when his dad, my Grandpa Thurmon, would sell it to him. The day it would be passed down to the next generation. This was his aspirations, and the desires of my dad's heart. But as the winds of adversity and strife would blow across these fields to our home, his heart would stop, and mine and my family's would break, before this dream would ever be realized.

SWS cranes at work on our dream home.

"My Grandparents went hungry to pay for this land. They paid the loan off in two years."

The Undoing

Part of my father's undoing was his childhood and his family relationships before I was born. But to understand more fully I must explain the historical points as they have been related to me by my mother and my grandparents, etc. My great-great grandpa, Will Mathis, originally leased farm land from DE Converse who built the Converse Cotton Mill. The land he leased is located on Dan River road and backs up to the Pacolet River. His son, Burnis, obtained the Steel Meadow Farm land from JT Blanton, Becks Branch, and the BH Smith Farm. Before being named Steel Meadow Farm, this property was referred to as the BH Mathis old home place. My grandfather bought it from his mother, Ida, in 1953. My great-grandfather Burnis died fairly young of what was believed to be a stroke. It was at this time that my grandpa Thurmon's mother, and his brothers and sisters agreed to sell him the farm for $74 per acre. My grandpa said his older brother Willie was a rounder, and a mechanic. Willie said he had no interest in the farm. So, my great-grandmother agreed to sell the farm to my grandpa. He was the youngest boy of the family. My grandpa Thurmon married Shirley Barnett. She said that my grandpa borrowed the money for the farm, and they went hungry to pay for it. Grandpa Thurmon worked as a mechanic during the day and farmed the land during the evenings and weekends. He told me that he paid for the 54 acres in two years time, by sowing the fields with wheat. As to his work ethic, I can certify that he was a Hoss of a man. Even into his mid-sixties he had biceps that would make an NFL linebacker or a lumberjack marvel. I remember as a child, and even as an 18-year-old man, seeing him step into a 20 acre corn or watermelon field in the early dawn, and hoe until the sun went down. He would eat corn in the field right off the stalk. He didn't take any breaks; he just kept working all day long.

I can never fully express what the impact of witnessing him work had on me as a young man. I guess subconsciously I was so moved by his determination and drive, it was inevitable that I aspired to become just like him. My grandpa always kept between 50 and 70 head of cows. Beef cows, that is, mostly Angus and white face. He was a mean old bird as I recall; all business with no toleration for foolishness. He looked at us grandchildren, I felt, as if we were terrorists or some form of pest, so he made sure he ran us out of his fields and barns. We knew to avoid him. He had problems with high blood pressure, and it wasn't very hard for us boys to have his head as red as a chili pepper, as we were inclined to trespass, loot, and pilfer through his tools, cow medicine, etc.

Grandpa Thurmon grew up the baby boy of seven children. I was always told that he was spoiled rotten by his sisters. My dad said that "Pa-pa" was very athletic and handsome in high school. He turned down a scholarship to Clemson for baseball and football. Grandpa said that they were poor, and there was no money to be made in sports in the 1940's, so he just went to work. However, my dad always felt as though my grandpa had to marry his mother, this contributed to this decision, and ultimately impacted how he treated him as a child.

The early years of my dad's childhood found Thurmon still dressing flashy, drinking alcohol, and gambling. My grandmother and the children suffered because

Shirley and Thurmon Mathis

of this. She told the story of the time when Thurmon went to the Rose Bowl game with his buddies during the winter months. She said my dad pulled some boards off the barn to burn in the fireplace to keep them from freezing. Grandpa got back from drinking and gambling for the weekend. He severely beat my dad for burning boards off the barn. She said the beating was so bad that she told my grandpa if he hit my dad again, she would call the police. My dad has two sisters he tried to protect and watch out after; their names are Cindy and Janis. My aunt Janis says she remembers putting her hands over her ears and running across the field to keep from hearing the beatings that my dad got from my Grandpa Thurmon.

I believe this to be the first of many triggers for my dad's emotional problems that manifested themselves as he would keep recollecting at times, all of his bad memories. My dad said he remembered that my grandpa had a light heart attack or panic attack at the Rose Bowl game. It was most likely gambling related. And, while my grandpa was recuperating, his Aunt Beonia brought groceries and Santa Claus to his mother. It was a heck of a way to figure out the Santa thing, I suppose. Another time later as my dad was a teenager, he tried out for the high school baseball team. My grandpa discovered him playing out in centerfield with no shoes on, as he didn't have any cleats. This embarrassed my grandpa, so he made him come off the field and whipped him all the way home. It was memories such as these that made my dad suffer from emotional problems. It became, as an adult for him, not be able to control his temper.

During my father's last year of high school, he was forced by his PE coach, Quay Farr, to box Harold Dean Rice, the high school bully. My dad remembered crying not wanting to have to fight him in the ring, but the coach forced him to. Much to everyone's amazement, including my dad, he beat the fool out of Harold Dean. Even though my dad was real stocky, he was extremely agile and fast with his hands. He discovered he could change situations with his fist. This fact helped him cultivate his violent nature. He was a good person with a great personality and heart. However, when put into a physical confrontation, somebody had better look out.

School soon became a burden for him, and with his negative home life, my dad decided to go into the Air Force early. He worked as an aircraft mechanic and was on the power lifting team. He was also involved in classified operations in Vietnam before it was called the Vietnam War. Some of what he saw there, as well as having his best friend killed when an airplane tire exploded, compelled my father to get out of the military. The Air Force gave him a medical discharge for emotional trauma. It was determined by the military doctors that my dad could go either way from a psychiatric standpoint. This information was unknown to us, and his immediate family, till after his death. Although, it was known by my grandmother and my grandpa, but they never mentioned it to us.

After the military, is when my dad met my mom and they decided to be married. Her name was Mary Ann Moore, my beautiful mother, of whom I previously mentioned in the beginning of this book. As my dad's business thrived, so did the level of stress and drug abuse. My daddy was a very physical man. He took all the vitamins and minerals he felt could help him maintain his energy. After years of working night and day he found local physicians, in Cowpens, to help him with energy and sleep. The doctors prescribed amphetamines for the daytime and sleeping pills for nighttime. It was the same treatment prescribed for stars such as Elvis Presley, and others who are on the go night and day with very little rest. It seems this drug regimen always ends up destroying the person it is intended to help. Amphetamines allow people to work incredible hours, while sleeping pills allow a person to sleep on demand. The roller coaster ride can destroy a person physically, emotionally, mentally, and spiritually. This, along with terrible bad luck, took its toll in a devastating way, upon my dad.

The Lord, in his infinite goodness and mercy, knew of the adversity that was headed our way, so he saw fit in 1978 to send two female missionaries from the Church of Jesus Christ of Latter-day Saints to our house one day. Those two young girls had walked holes in their shoes trying to spread the message of Jesus Christ, and the "Restoration" of the gospel. As they began to talk it seemed as if the church was not something new to my father. It turned out that my great-grandmother Fannie Barnett was converted to the church despite great persecution from the people of Cowpens. After she joined the church and people started complaining about it, my great grandfather, Robert Tuck Barnett, told her that she could not go to church anymore with the Mormons. She remained faithful, nonetheless, and walked every Sunday to the main street of Cowpens just to waive at the missionaries and members as they drove by on their way to church.

This had a very negative impact on her daughter, my grandmother Shirley. My grandmother told me that she hated the church because of the trouble that it caused in her family. She said, however, that one weekend while my grandpa was away drinking and gambling two missionaries came by the farm. My father was very young and very sick. My grandmother was very worried about how sick he was. The missionaries asked if they could give him a blessing and pray for him so my grandmother reluctantly agreed and thought that it couldn't hurt. She said what happened next changed her life and put her on the path to accepting the gospel. She related that as the missionaries prayed for her sick little boy, that the prayer was so very beautiful. She said everything that she would want them to say, they said and more. She accepted and agreed to read *The Book of Mormon*.

When the neighbors found out and word spread that she was reading *The Book of Mormon*, the people of the town told my grandfather that he should take the children away from her; that she had lost her mind! She recalled how one day the ladies of the local church came to her door to pay her a visit. She said they began to argue with her and to scream at her. She said they kept saying we have a Bible; there can be no more Bible! There is only one bible! And that *The Book of Mormon* was not true. She said she ran upstairs and threw herself on the bed and started to cry. She remembered all the trouble the church had caused for her family. She said she grabbed *The Book of Mormon* and opened it, not knowing whether to rip it, or throw it out the window. She said when she looked at the words on the open page, that she realized it was exactly the words that the women were shouting at her. She had opened to the book of Nephi where the Savior says in the last day there shall be many who will say, "A Bible, a Bible, there can be no more Bible!" She said she knew then that the church was true, so she joined and was baptized. She remained a faithful member for some 20 years before my grandfather decided to change his life and be baptized. She said the missionaries came one day and taught my grandfather the gospel all day and all night. And when the next day came my grandfather decided to join the church. He gave up all his habits, cigarettes, and gave his life to Christ, and never fell away or lost his new found faith.

They were devout Mormons for some 15 to 20 years before that fateful day that the sister missionaries showed up at our door. It was a fact that I was not aware of. My mother had always carried us to the Methodist Church, and I was a member of it. I am truly grateful for that beautiful summer day when those missionaries showed up at our door. I remember how I jumped to my feet as a boy of 14 years of age, and said aloud, "I Knew It! I knew there had to be more!" This I said, as they told of the restoration of the Church of Jesus Christ, of how the Father and His only Begotten Son appeared to Joseph Smith, Junior, in a sacred grove. How this happened when he prayed also at the age of 14. My heart jumped within me at the sound of truth. The Holy Ghost bore witness of this truth to me.

Many people have sometimes looked back at their life and been able to identify a turning point or a pivot point that made them who they are. My defining, moment, was 100%, with no doubt, my coming to the knowledge that the Lord himself had once again restored His church back to its fullness here on earth. It was, and is to this day, the reason that I live, love, hope, and dream. The miracle of my obtaining a testimony of *The Book of Mormon*, and the latter-day prophet, has been the rock of my salvation. It has given me a relationship and understanding of Jesus Christ that could not be obtained by any other way, or by any other source. It has brought me as a boy, and as a man, through the tremendous hailstorms of life. It has also sustained me through the hell and anguish associated with the Steel Meadow Farm. I am a perfect example of my Savior's love and His ability to make anything beautiful, any life happy, and at peace.

Robert Little Tuck
and
Fannie Estelle Morrow Barnette

Burnis H. Mathis   **Ida Millwood Mathis**

Beginning to Write, Again
September 12, 2008

My Hunting Journal

So much of my life has changed since I last wrote in this book. After all, of the many crazy events of my life, and after the last year that I've had, I realize that life is like a river. That even on the peaceful sunny days, it is changing. It may not appear so, but nevertheless, little by little, life is always changing, always flowing into the future, looking forward and never looking back. As I find myself secluded in a hunting camp in Malaad City Idaho, high in the mountainous elk country, I realize just how stressed out, and depressed my life has become. I have suddenly had to come to grips with being totally isolated and alone in these mountains, with no cell phone reception. I am learning to calm down and learning the healing effects of squeezing a stress ball.

September 13, 2008

I got to talk to Angela and Alex today. I love my family so much. I can't wait to get home. I pray that I do. I do not enjoy flying too much. I almost shot a 5x5 elk today! He bugled about 50 yards from me. He came walking straight toward me and suddenly ducked behind a large cedar tree.

Moments later, he bolted and ran. I could not get a shot with my bow and arrow, but he was so very impressive, I was in awe of his beauty.

September 14, 2008

Hunting in the a.m.

Saw nothing. I wish I was home.

I miss my wife and kids.

I am terribly out of shape!

I have to lose weight!

I cannot express how much I miss my family!

I hope that they are doing well.

The high altitude, and rocky mountains, is very challenging.

I hope my family went to church today and hope they are doing well back in South Carolina.

Sunset at Malaad, Idaho

September 15, 2008

I climbed to the top of Monument Mountain this morning at 5 AM. I cannot believe I made it to the top! I placed a stone on top of the Monument. The Monument is simply a pile of rocks at the very top of the mountain. My rock will remain there as a testament that I was there! This rocky mountain Idaho country is so very beautiful. I got a camera today and began taking pictures. I wish my family could see this place. Maybe someday they will. Troy, Rex, and myself, were the only ones to summit to the top of the mountain. We saw some elk run into the South Pocket Canyon, where I came so close to shooting the 5x5 elk two days ago. One of the elk we saw today was very huge. He was so massive he couldn't keep up with the rest of the herd. I would love to bag him. To sit high in these mountains and listen to the wind blowing through the sagebrush, pine trees, and aspens, is really, overwhelming. I will go home a changed man forever! I have been able to see myself in such a profound way. I realize just how bad my health and emotions have become. I realize that I have been acting and reacting to fear. If I'm privileged to make it back home, that will change! I intend to take this calm feeling of the mountains back home with me. I miss my family and it's only Monday.

September 15, 2008 Afternoon Hunt

Troy's dad came to camp this afternoon. It was a joy for me to see Troy get to hug his dad. He is a very nice man in his 70s and he gets around pretty good. It is apparent from his shaking frame that he has done a lot of hard work. It is good to watch Troy and all his brothers and dad together. They dressed him in camouflage and Troy rode him on a four-wheeler where we were going to hunt. Going into the South Pocket I had feeling to knock an arrow, and sure enough Troy and Rex jumped two huge mule deer that came running straight to me. I drew my arrow back, but decided not to kill either deer, even though they stopped right in front of me. I didn't want to mess up the elk hunt for Troy and his dad. I can't help but be sad over the fact that my Dad is gone. So many good years he missed; well maybe we both did. I felt close to my grandpa Thurmon, high in the mountains yesterday. I miss my dad today. Sometimes I feel he is near to me. I just want to go home and be with my family. Five days down, five to go. I will try to kill something tomorrow; today was a day of mercy. I do not see how Troy can live so far from his family. He lives with me in the great state of South Carolina. Over 2000 miles from Idaho!

September 16, 2008 Tuesday

Morning hunt was nothing remarkable, just two coyotes screaming at me. Saw two mule deer again on the opposite mountaintop. Troy is acting like a punk. I'm ready to go home.

Evening hunt. I got set up in the catch pond area. Didn't see anything. I got to meditate and pray a lot. Saw a huge mule deer right about dark. I hope to ice him in the morning; it was just too dark to get a good shot. I can't wait to be home kissing baby doll. I am missing my family.

September 17, 2008

Morning hunt. This hunt went okay. I went by myself again, and that's the way I like it. Troy took all three guides with him, again. I hope he kills an elk for his own sanity. I didn't see my big buck, but this country is so very beautiful, and the hills are so challenging. I'm trying to be careful, so I don't get hurt. The others don't know where I'm hunting, so they would have a hard time finding me if something happened. I miss Angela, Casey, Catelyn, Connor, Alex, Cross, and my bed!

Evening hunt. Rode around the canyons looking for elk while watching Steve Cooper and Rex Williams drink one beer after another. Fun, fun, fun! I wish I was at home eating ice cream with my kids. No rain, dusty, and miserable, but hanging in there.

September 18, 2008
Thursday Morning

Went hunting and slipped off the side of the first draw we came across. I set up and hid halfway down the hill. I got overrun by another hunter who had the same idea as me. After he went on his way, three buck deer came my way. I shot at the first one, but apparently the arrow hit, and broke off the barbed wire fence. The arrowhead cut the strand in two. I didn't kill the deer, but it was very, very exciting, and thrilling. Got to speak to Cross and Angela today! I love to speak to my son and to hear his voice. The sound of my wife's voice made me feel very needy. Can't wait to get home and see my family. I pray they are safe.

September 18, 2008 Evening Hunt

Went to the "Onion" Canyon today. Saw lots of signs, walked a lot. Did not see one elk. Rex, Heffer, Hubbert, and Steve Cooper all enjoyed the beer. It's real serious hunting around here! I am so ready for the airplane. I miss my family. I talked to Angela and she said she has me a surprise. I hope so!

September 19, 2008 Morning Hunt

It's really, cold again. We got up at 5 AM and rode the four wheelers to the mountain. I let a little two point buck slide today. He walked up within 25 feet of me and just stared at me. He then took off screaming and alerted the other big deer of my presence, so I didn't get them. Oh well, it's getting close to going home. Troy got to sit in a really good spot. He shot and missed the elk. That went over like a box of rocks! Things are out of control. I miss my home.

September 19, 2008 Evening Hunt

I tried to take a nap but could not. Too much mouth, and blaring rock 'n roll music. Steve Cooper wanted to know what I was writing about in my journal. We talked about Clay. We talked about church and my friend Scott Ponder's murder case.

Troy, Steve, and Rex

A spectacle with Troy and the hunt tonight. He was dressed in two layers of camouflage, and looked like he was going to war in Vietnam! Troy getting to kill an elk is driving him crazy. I shot a spike elk and I know that I hit it tonight!

He ran away and it got dark. Maybe we will find it in the morning. Well, it's about 10 PM tonight and the night owls and the rock music, just gets louder, and louder. I absolutely cannot wait to get the heck out of Idaho and back home.

September 20, 2008 Morning Hunt
Last day
Thank you Jesus

There was no morning hunt. Troy and Rex slipped off silently to go alone. I know they needed time alone. I went by myself to look for the elk, I didn't find my arrow.

I hope the elk I shot is dead, and not suffering.

When I finally get back home, I will not be suffering.

Going back, Walking through Hell...

Date unknown

I have begun to write the story of Steel Meadow Farm, again. It is very difficult to do. I usually write when I'm on vacation with my family. It seems that's the only time that I can bring myself to do it. It is there, surrounded by their love and the pounding of the ocean, that my memories not only can be unlocked, but faced again, as well. And, with that being said, we will begin again.

I can still hear, the sound of my mother's scream, as she slammed the phone down on the receiver. Amidst her wailing and crying, I was able to make out those terrible words of, "It's your daddy, he's been shot!"

I guess it's the pure adrenaline and fear that hits you so hard, that you feel as though you are no longer in your body. This was the case, at this time for me. It was like I was outside myself, watching myself. Three different times during the next 20 minutes, I felt sick feelings coming over me. It was taking the life out of me, it seemed. At each time I got down on my knees and begged my Heavenly Father to spare my dad's life; to let him live long enough for me to be able to tell him once more that I loved him. We found out when we got to the hospital the ambulance had stopped three separate times because my dad's heart had stopped, so they had to pull over to revive him. I feel he stayed alive as a result of those prayers.

That day came one week before my 18th birthday. Now I am soon to be 44 years old. I can tell you that the memories have not faded. Dr. Keller was the brain surgeon on call. He had been a good friend of my daddy and the family. He came in the waiting room of the hospital to give us the news. He said that daddy had been shot in the top back of his head. The bullet took a downward path and split, going different directions in his brain. Part of the bullet would be irretrievable. He said that daddy had about a 10% chance to make it through the night. In my mind, I initially thought my daddy must've been shot in the back. I never imagined it would be in the head.

The Hospital

During the next 8 to 10 hours I sat with my heart in my throat. The hard chairs in the intensive care waiting room were very unforgiving, to say the least. I can always remember the elevator doors coming open with more and more people. Folks were hanging around to hear the news that Steve Mathis was dead. The people of the town of Cowpens kept a vigil, waiting to get the word, that the man who had done so much, and given so much, might be human after all. Many of the faces visiting the hospital were people who I knew owed him money. So great, and so tragic, so intense, were the feelings of despair that I felt as if I were dying. With every ounce of energy of my soul, I concentrated and prayed, holding on somehow to my dad's life. I tried to imagine the intense pain that he had to be suffering. I knew he was in agony. I knew he was scared. So horrific are the scenes in my mind. The .38 caliber Colt pistol that daddy was shot with, made his head and face look like he had been hit with a sledgehammer. He was unrecognizable, yet somehow, he continued to breathe, somehow, he continued to fight.

Looking at my dad in the hospital bed it reminded me of the pictures I'd seen of him when I was a child. It made me think of the terrible beating that he took at the hands of the Cantrell boys, of whom he had fired from working for him. The two disgruntled employees made up a plan to attack my father one night after he closed his welding shop. They beat his head and face in with a pipe wrench. His face and nasal passages had to be reconstructed. All the years of him battling hay-fever, sinus headaches, welding smoke, and dust. Now to be suffering from a gunshot wound to the head, it was just unbearable for me. My soul screamed within me.

With my all, I cried and prayed, and asked God why? Why, Why, God Why? My dad was my hero. I knew of his goodness. I witnessed his kindness. I felt his mercy. I knew who he was before the drugs, and before the business failures. It was just too much to see him suffer this way. So much talent, so many accomplishments, so many friends, and now fighting for his life in a Neurological Intensive Care unit. How the road had led to this place was astonishing to me. It did not seem real, yet it was reality.

As time went on in the hospital day by day, hour by hour, minute by minute, I waited for the ten minute visit, which came every three hours. It was at that time I would try to get Daddy to squeeze my hand. As he clung to life, the doctors would say things like, his movements are involuntary, he is going to be in a vegetative state, he will be a paraplegic, and he will have no movement other than the right arm. But I knew in my heart that daddy was aware and trying to let me know he heard my voice. As it turns out, I was right!

Time went on, hours at a time, and daddy suddenly began to open his eyes. For two weeks I stayed at the hospital refusing to leave. There was a parking deck being constructed that I could see outside of the sixth floor window of the hospital. I couldn't help but think that my dad should be erecting the concrete slabs and doing that project himself. He had put up and erected the steel and concrete for shopping malls, hospitals, schools, and industry around the community and various states. The fact was at one time, and not too long ago, Steve's Welding Service was the biggest independent steel erector in the southeast. How it had come to be just one man in critical condition, with a gunshot wound to the head, was just unbelievable to me.

After two weeks, the crowds began to dissipate. It appeared that daddy would live. He would be confined to a wheelchair, completely paralyzed from the neck down, except for the use of his right arm. Amazingly, he was conscious and responsive. He came a long way from being shot in the head, to now trying to speak to everyone. His mind was clear. The only things that he ever said to me was, "Son, it ain't nothing but pain!" He said, "They must have broken my arm when I fell," as if he had been fighting with someone. He said, "I love you, too, son." That is what meant the most to me; it was the only thing that was important! I told him I loved him, and he said he loved me!

He never said how he got shot. The doctors were afraid he would get upset if he tried to talk too much. We all knew he was shot in the back of the head. The bullet had taken a downward path. He either committed suicide, it was an accident, or someone killed him; we will never know. There was only one fingerprint on the gun, and it was NOT his!

Approximately two weeks after my dad was shot, on a sunny Sunday afternoon, my dad died. On February 5, 1984 Steve Mathis began to pass blood clots from his legs. My mother visited him in the hospital that day. My dad was upset and told my mother to make the man dressed in white leave the room. She tried to explain to my father that there was no one in the room with her, but he was convinced there was, and that the man wanted him to go with him. After that, my dad passed the first blood clot. The nurses revived him, and the doctor told my mother they would try everything possible to keep it from happening again. My dad asked her to go and get his boys! He asked my grandpa to go and call his attorney and tell him to come. My Mom said he looked scared after the first blood clot moved to his heart.

On the way to the hospital, once again I began to experience the overwhelming sickening feeling that daddy was dying. I remember the chaplain meeting us at the elevator. We were about fifteen minutes too late. The third blood clot lodged in his heart. And as his heart had stopped, my heart would forevermore be torn to pieces.

Like a sail on a ship shredded by hurricane winds, my heart will always bear the scars of the Steel Meadow Farm. It is a storm that continues to rage to this day. I can only dream of peaceful sunny shores. Will it ever be?

Dad is on the left.

The Funeral

I can remember full-well the first time I failed my mother. It was when the chaplain told her that she would have to view and identify my dad's body after he died. I just could not bring myself to go back there with her. I remember her weeping and asking why his eyes were still open. At that point, I looked at the sixth- floor window of the building at the end of the hall. My heart was beating wildly. I could see myself running as fast as I could and jumping through it and falling to the pavement below. I wanted to die in an effort to go with him. I wanted to go, too! It was at that moment I looked down at my baby brother Clay. He was only 12-years-old. I realized I had to remain strong for him. I put my arm around him and said, "It's going to be okay!"

How I wish I could have somehow made that promise come true. It seems as though that was be too big of a challenge; too much weight and too much responsibility. It was made very apparent over the years that a tree cannot stand if the trunk is hewn down. And a family can't survive when a father is hewn down.

It started to snow the evening of my father's death. I can recall walking around the barbed wire fences of Steel Meadow Farm calling his name over and over. We had a mare horse that had done the same thing after its colt died. She went around and around the fence neighing to no avail. It dawned on me that I was doing the exact same thing. I realized then what grief is. It is the acute, unbearable awareness of something or someone being ripped from your universe.

While at the hospital, I had whittled an ironworker's spud wrench from a wooden 2 x 4 from the construction site of their new parking deck. I whittled while I sat all those hours in the hospital. I placed it in dad's right hand, in his coffin. The autopsy people sawed his head in half to retrieve the bullet fragments. They did not do a great job putting the pieces back together. He looked like something out of a

Frankenstein movie. What a sight for his kids and family to see! Still, it was my dad in his suit and cowboy boots. It hurt so very much to say goodbye.

There was a tremendous crowd at the funeral. I sang, "How Great Thou Art." I was a pallbearer. It was a very surreal sight to see all of Dad's, "lead men," and employees carry him to his grave. They all wept, for they knew he made them professional ironworkers and crane operators. They knew he loved them enough to see them become their potential. Before they covered up the casket, my two younger brothers Clint and Clay took all the money they had in their pockets, all their loose change, and threw it in the grave. Looking back, now 25-years later, it seems so symbolic, because they have always continued to throw their lives and their money away. It is as if their lives and ambitions ended at that funeral as well.

The Aftermath

I wish I could write that somehow we were all able to move on or to go forward to live a happy life after that terrible event. But I cannot, for it is not so. The years would pass away. Time would move forward. But for so many members of my family, the nightmare would not end. The tragedy, the despair, depression, and drugs would raise its ugly head, time and time again.

A quintet of elders from our church sang, "*A Poor Wayfaring man of Grief,*" at the funeral. It was truly a moving song. It was the song Joseph Smith sang before the angry mob burst through the door of the Carthage Jail in Missouri, and shot him dead. I remember looking at my bereaved mother of 38-years of age. Sitting beside her was my girlfriend, Angela Gilbert. She was a very, very, pretty, green eyed girl. She lived in the same house, slept in the same room as my mother did at the time my dad started dating her. How is that for coincidence? As they sang that song, the voice of the Lord said unto my soul, "Behold thy family!" It was not an audible voice, but it was a voice spoken by the power of the Holy Ghost to my heart. I knew then, that Angela Gilbert was to be my wife.

That was in fact the greatest blessing that ever came into my life. On the saddest day of my life, the Lord spoke from the heavens to my heart, and gave me a key; a key to happiness. It was not that He took away my pain, my scars, and my stripes, but He did grant unto me the key of knowledge. Knowledge that if I obeyed Him, He would bring me joy, and help me experience peace in this life.

As I write the words of this book beside the ocean at Ocean Lakes, Myrtle Beach, South Carolina, the sky is blue. The sun and sand are hot. The seagulls sing and play, and Angela Gilbert Mathis the mother of my five children, my girlfriend, and my wife, still sits beside me. She is still very, very, beautiful. She is reading a book by Nicholas Sparks. As I look across the ocean and ponder over the events of my life and Steel Meadow Farm, I am so humbly moved and thankful that I listened, that I heard, and that I obeyed the voice of the Holy Ghost as it said to me that terrible day, "Behold thy family!"

"Behold, thy family."

The Apostasy

My father baptized my mom and little brothers into the Church of Jesus Christ of Latter Day Saints. It was during the time of the booming of his business, SWS, and about the same time that construction began on "The House." All seemed so well, everything and everyone seemed to be healthy and happy. I can remember my dad bear solemn testimony in church, of his love for his family, the truthfulness of *The Book of Mormon*, and its latter-day prophet. I can remember the unfortunate events of his business that began to take a very stressful toll on him and our family.

You see, my dad erected the steel at two major hospitals at the same time. One located in Cherokee, North Carolina, and the other in Augusta, Georgia. He never was paid for the work done on either of them. In both cases the general contractor filed for bankruptcy and did not pay his debt. The Cherokee National Hospital was built on an Indian reservation, and technically isn't even a part of the United States of America. As far as the federal court systems are concerned, the reservation is pretty much run by the Tribal Council. My dad was sold out by his lifelong friend and attorney who had handled the case for him. When it came time to go to trial his attorney declined to go. My dad had to find additional counsel. My dad felt betrayed by this attorney. He helped this attorney get established. Dad helped to get him elected Mayor of Cowpens. This attorney had served as his bishop as well, during the black, dark times. He had become, over time, a state senator, but when my dad needed him the most he chose not to be there.

The judge in Cherokee, North Carolina, told my father during the trial that he needed his ass kicked for letting the Cherokees owe him that much money in the first place! Losing that case was devastating both to my dad, and his business. The Augusta hospital job was also tied up in federal court. It was still under appeal when my dad died. It was there in Augusta that my dad had his first employee killed on the job. Mark Kenlaw fell 110 feet down an elevator shaft. He and a couple more employees went up to the top of the steel frame building at lunch time, undoubtedly to show off for the candy stripers who would watch them from the windows of the completed hospital wing.

Mark stood up on an I-beam to act like he was hammering something to get their attention. As he swung the hammer down between his legs, he lost his balance, and fell down the elevator shaft to his death.

My dad was a changed man after that. I remember the day he got the call. One of his men was killed on the job. He ran to get into his El Camino and sped down the highway to Augusta. Shortly after that he had two more men fall off the iron and get hurt, because of their own negligence. One of the men broke his neck, and the other broke his back. They had connected an I-beam to a vertical column. After they had welded it off in place, they signaled the crane operator to let down on the cable. They had not applied enough welds onto the beam to support its weight. The crane let down. The two men took off the support cables before completing the weld. The two young, foolish, iron workers went for the ride of their lives, when their welds broke loose, and they tumbled to the ground.

After that, Steve's Welding Service worker's compensation insurance went to $800 per day to finish the job. To endure this setback, and to pay for room and board for family members of the ones involved in accidents, and then to not get paid for the job! My father died abandoned by his attorney, with both cases tied up in the federal court of appeals. Every time Steve's Welding Service would win a decision, the big companies would appeal the case. This would postpone the trial and hearing for years. In the process, my dad had spent all of his liquid assets on finishing those large projects. He had to face bankruptcy and failure in his small town. He lost his cranes, the shop, the tools, and most importantly, his pride. He was forced to take out a mortgage on the house. Even though he paid cash for the construction of the house, and it had no debt, he took out a mortgage to pay all corporate taxes to the

IRS. He managed to keep one hydraulic 35-ton Lorain crane by putting it in my Grandma Nell Moore's name. He still had it when he died.

Ultimately, it all boils down to what you stand for. This life has a way of letting you reap what you sow. The noble employees of my dad, the ones who loved him in return for the love he showed them, went on to become the best in their profession. They became lead men, foremen, supervisors, crane operators, etc. The ones who were not noble, the wicked, hard hearted, and thieves, went on to a life of drug abuse and shame. Some of them overdosed on drugs. Some were shot. Some went to prison. Some drank alcohol and smoked themselves to death. The attorney that let my dad, my mother, and us three brothers down, ultimately was disbarred and convicted of bank fraud. He was excommunicated from the church, divorced, and estranged by his family in a most publicly humiliating way. Yes, it is true; we all reap what we sow, for God will not be mocked.

During the hardest times of watching his business go up in flames, my dad was fighting a spiritual battle between good and evil, and between truth and deceit. Christ-like love versus violence. I saw my dad in humble prayer pleading with the Lord to rescue him from these enemies. I don't know if he ever realized that his biggest enemy was himself. Was it that he never felt good enough for his dad? Was it the beatings that he suffered as a child that made him respond to things so violently? In the end, it all boiled down to pride. It was the pride that existed between my dad and my mom, making the situation for both of them unbearable. It was pride that cost them their happiness.

The Lord had provided a way for my dad to escape the financial burdens of his business. It came when he began to move machinery for Milliken & Company. It would have been, and could have been, and should have been, a golden opportunity to rig and erect textile equipment in the south. Because of the southern textile industry, people over the years made fortunes doing this type of work. But because of the pride of my grandparents, who both worked for Clarkson Brothers, a rigging company doing the same thing, they both insisted that my dad not do any more work for Milliken and Company. My dad tried to convince his mother and father to quit their jobs and work for him, but they would not, and chose to keep their positions with Clarkson Brothers. Because of their pressure, they persuaded him to stop rigging and hauling textile machinery, and my dad continued to struggle. It would be astonishing to my grandparents 20 years later, to see that opportunity and its financial blessings reemerge for SWS!

My mom and dad were separated when he got shot. Several years of bankruptcy court and financial stresses, had enabled them to become estranged. Because of pride my dad began to rely on sleeping pills and barbiturates to help him cope. He began to gamble on professional sports to try and make ends meet. The pressures of this kind of life and the looming debt of Steel Meadow Farm began to be great.

Sometimes he would come home covered in blood from fighting. Sometimes bullets grazed him when a poker game went bad or from people attempting to rob him of what he won. This was very upsetting and traumatizing to little boys who loved and idolized their dad. We always had a fear that he was going to get hurt.

Anyhow, that's when bad times went to worse. Dad and mom kept fighting. Dad kept pulling outward and away. I recall seeing endless days that he slept on the couch, all day. As a child I never saw him at home much. He always left early and came home late. Now he just slept. He would dress up at night like a cowboy to go gamble and do whatever.

The first signs of real trouble came one afternoon. I got home from school and I knew that my dad was not acting right. He was lying in the bathtub with only his nose sticking out of the water. He appeared to be asleep. I spoke to him calling his name. He tried to answer, but his speech was slurred. I could hardly understand him. He tried to get out of the bath tub, and fell out of it on to the floor. He seemed to be having difficulty breathing. As a young teenager I can't remember who I called first. I knew he had taken too much of something, medicine wise. And whatever it was, it was shutting his body down. I grabbed him and pulled him up on his knees. I put his head over the commode and told him to hang on. I got a pot from the kitchen and began to pour cold water over his head and back. This seemed to startle him, and that was exactly the result I was trying to get. He would seem to become aware, only to fade back out again. I did this until the medical personnel arrived. I don't recall how many Tuinal he had taken, but he had to have his stomach pumped out at the hospital. The doctor said I probably saved his life. I was just glad he was going to live.

My mom and grandparents, Thurmon and Shirley, brought my dad back from the emergency room that evening. My dad was lying on the couch when they got him home. My mom and grandmother Shirley began to try and ask him why? What was he thinking? The first thing he said was, "Because, I ain't got no money." At this, my grandpa threw his nose up in the air and said, "WHEEW!" The second thing my dad said was the same statement I heard him say several years previously when he had a nervous breakdown at the Mathis family reunion at my great-aunt Pauline's house. He said, "Nobody really loves me." When he said this my grandpa began laughing at him and said, "Oh boy!" It was at this point that my heart burst inside of me! I could feel my dad dying inside. I could feel the weight, and the pain. I jumped to my feet and shouted at my grandpa, "No wonder he is like he is, with a dad like you! You are just an old son of a %!*^#!"

Upon this, my grandfather, who was still very much of a man physically, jumped up to hit me. I shouted to him, "Bring your sorry ass outside," as I went through the house. And yes, he came after me! My maternal grandmother, Nellie Moore, God rest her beautiful soul, I don't know where she had come from in the house, but she jumped in front of my grandpa with a broom in her hands. She drew that broomstick back like a baseball bat, and said, "Old man Mathis, you lay one hand on that boy and I'll bust your brains out all over this back porch step!" At this he looked shocked. Grandpa said, "He ain't going to cuss my mommy!" Papa was the baby child and loved his mommy like no other. My granny Nell just looked at him and said, "You hush, you old fool, now get your ass outta here." My grandmother Shirley said, Thurmon it's time to go, right now! That was the beginning of hatred between grandpa Thurmon and me that would last for some 15 years. More on that later.

Later on that night, as the wee hours of the morning came calling, I heard my mom yell for me. Daddy got a hold of more pills that he had hidden in the bedroom. Once again, he was fading out fast. I remember running outside to the edge of our road with a flashlight. The moon was full, and the frost was thick, as I stood outside with no shirt, only my shorts. I could hear the sirens coming, they seemed so far away. Finally, the ambulance arrived, and as the paramedics worked with my dad, and he kept pulling the bed sheet covers over his face saying, "I want to see Jesus. I want to see his face. I want to ask him why He did me this way." Dad survived the second overdose attempt. My Uncle, Lewis Moore, said that he was crying out for help. I guess we all knew it was so, but no one knew who could help him. There was no one, but God.

TRIBUTE

The following pictures are tribute to my father, Stephen Terry Mathis (1942-1984) and all of the original 'Steve's Welding' personnel. It was their true grit and determination that inspired me to become as one of them True Craft Professionals.

A special thanks to each one for being patient and allowing a young boy to observe and take notes.

July 2010

Dad eventually moved out. We saw less and less of him. We lived in fear; fear of him never coming back, fear of what it would be like if he did. My mother died a slow spiritual death inside. Nights on end, knowing that Daddy was off doing God knows what, ate away at her soul. At the same time, three young boys began to get more and more out of control. There were many nights that I would lay in bed listening to the sound of my mother crying. I did not know what to say. I did not know what to do. I felt so incredibly sorry for her.

All I wanted as a boy was to be just like my dad. I let my love for him blind me as to anything he did wrong. If dad drank a little white lightning every once in a while then it was okay for me to try it, too. If dad had a briefcase full of medicine and speed, then it must be okay for me to try a little of it. The picture wasn't too pretty. It's a wonder that I didn't get in real serious trouble. Daddy discovered that I was drinking on a few occasions, and he and mom would blame each other. I remember taking speed about the age of 17, out of his briefcase and staying up all day, and night, and day. I was as nervous as a cat rubbed backward! My heart was pounding, and I was sweating so bad, I whittled all night with my pocket knife. I cut every finger I had, and taped them up with pieces of electrical tape. My dad saw me and knew I was messed up. He and mom confronted me. It was outside in the yard at dusk. As usual, dad and mom started trading insults. He kept pressing me to admit it, and wanted to know why and what I was taking. I couldn't take it anymore, I started to cry and explained to him that I hated the way things were. That I had seen all the things he had gone through, how hard he had worked, and I told him that I loved him. I remember, and can never forget, seeing the shock and fear in his eyes when I shouted at him, "#*#^* It! I WANT TO BE JUST LIKE YOU!" I think he realized then that I was following right behind him in every single footstep. At that statement dad and mom began fighting again, screaming at each other, and then he finally got in his truck and left.

We rarely saw daddy much after that. Clay would call him, and make arrangements to stay at his hotel room some nights on the weekends, but that didn't happen too often. Clint would talk to him on the phone and help him pick teams to bet on. Mom began to work a job in Cowpens, in an effort to feed us boys. The fact that she had to go to work caused my dad a lot of jealousy and mental issues. It was just more public humiliation for him to deal with. But she had no choice, while dad was away living a life of sin with his newfound girlfriend; mom needed a way to feed her and three teenage boys. It was not an easy task. I don't know how she was able to listen to all the ugly comments that people all over town would make to her about having to work. To all of the questions and comments as to why "the house" was not finished yet, etc. I guess over all she must've cried an ocean of tears, maybe more. But, I do know this; she always put herself last, to make sure our needs were met. She did not care what the townspeople thought, did, or said. She managed to work and find a way to keep our little home, in front of the mansion house, full of something to eat, and with the power on.

I remember one of the last times I saw my dad was during the cold winter months between the end of 1983, and the beginning of 1984. I just remember it being really cold. We ran out of heating oil, and mom had asked dad to come relight the furnace. He came over cussing. Thank goodness mother wasn't home. After he got the furnace lit, he said, "I'm going to move back home and straighten this #*X* place out!" If only he would have made good on that promise his life would have been spared and changed. But he never made good on that promise.

He made another surprise visit earlier in the summer to find one of my high school friends, who I ran around with, using his chainsaw. I was at football practice. My mom had offered to pay my friend Billy to help her clean up the yard and cut down some bushes. She was a very beautiful woman and my dad had a lot of jealousy issues, and crazy thoughts. He got outraged over the saw and kicked Billy in his butt as he snatched the chainsaw away. A 17-year-old boy! He accused mom of wearing short shorts and trying to seduce Billy. They began to shout and before she really knew what was happening my dad was hitting her in the face with his fist. She broke free from him somehow and ran down the road to the barn where my grandpa was. Her face was busted up really bad. He took her by the arm and led her back up the road to my dad, and said to him, "You did it, and you can fix it." She was badly beaten. She was scared and terrified of daddy, so she broke free from grandpa and ran over to our next-door neighbor's house and screamed for them. The neighbor pulled a rifle on dad and made him get out of the yard.

My mom had to have plastic surgery on her face. I remember going to the hospital and looking at her in her bloody clothes. Seeing her beautiful face beaten in, I was so very mad at my dad. When my mom got home from having her face all stitched up, I saw daddy coming up the road in his Ranchero. I ran and got my gun. I had an 11 gauge Remington automatic shotgun that he had bought me for my birthday some years ago. He pulled in, down at the front of our driveway, and just sat there looking at me holding that shotgun. I prayed he didn't come up the driveway and get out. I knew that if he did, I was going to shoot him. I loved my dad, but I hated him for what he did to my mom. I hated that dark side, the violent side of him that was so explosive. I hated him for putting me in this situation. Right then, I would be forced to shoot him. He backed out of the driveway after a 10-minute stare down with me. It was the biggest relief of my life. I know it was the biggest burden of his.

I know my dad loved my mother more than anything. I know he would've done anything to make it all go away, but he couldn't. He could not change the mistakes he had made. He couldn't undo the endless woes of his business. He couldn't let go of his pride. He couldn't make things right with my mom. He couldn't know that his life would be cut so short, that he would miss out on another lifetime of his family and grandchildren he would never see here on earth. He couldn't save himself, from himself.

My mind goes back to that cold February day. February 5, 1984. The day that my father died, it was so hard to believe that he was actually gone. There would be no Mormon mission for me to serve. There would be no playing football for college. There would be no joining the Air Force. My mission would be to stay at home with the family.

The Exodus

During my dad's funeral a few of his rogue acquaintances took the liberty to rob his remaining tools from the basement of our new house. My grandpa accused us boys of having something to do with it. It was just the beginning of all the harsh words between us boys and grandpa.

To watch one's family tossed and turned, to be torn apart continually upon the rough seas of adversity, is such a defeating thing. You feel helpless. But as time and years would reveal, once the anchor has torn loose, the ship will be dashed upon the rocks. As you see, my grandpa was made executor of my dad's will. It was left solely up to him as to how to liquidate my dad's estate.

The first thing he did was to have my dad's equipment appraised by three of the most crooked men in the south. After they appraised the equipment, they immediately submitted a check to my grandpa and purchased everything. As unbelievable as it sounds, it is true. But this is only the beginning, as my grandpa attempted to settle my dad's estate, anyone that could muster up a tear, and say my dad owed them something, was paid, "Johnny on the spot." No questions asked. It became a joke around Cowpens. It was such a miserable time in my family's life. And to have every conman and drug addict in the country, showing up to hustle my grandpa out of the estate money was just too much! Some of my dad's most trusted friends, and people whom he had helped establish their own businesses, were the very ones who came like wolves for the blood of the lamb. They simply had no regard for the Widow Mathis or her three boys.

One day soon a big truck came from across the front yard, it did not use the driveway. My mother asked, "Can I help you?" The man, Mr. Rich Tyrant said, "Can you help me? Hell, I own this place now. I bought it from Mr. Mathis for $50,000."

We found out we would be forced to move away from our little white farmhouse and the Steel Meadow Farm.

Great-Grandma planted a seed to grow this Magnolia tree.

She proudly stands on the left side of the entrance to the farm's property.

Today it's nearly four-stories tall.

Time tests each of us.

Ida's Magnolia tree

reminds us to appreciate

our family roots.

The lovely scent, in its season, brings

our lives closer together on the

Steel Meadow Farm.

A Promise

I remember as an eighteen-year-old kid watching a bulldozer demolish our little white, wooden, two-bedroom house. It didn't take long, but it seemed like an eternity flashed before my eyes. Each time the bulldozer pushed down more of the house more memories came down with it. I loved that little house. It will always be home to me. I remember promising myself as I watched the destruction that someday, somehow, I would get it back. I promised my brothers, who were watching beside me that day, I would get it back! How, I did not know, but I promised myself I would.

It's funny how quickly that promise faded into the worries of the week, the months, and the years ahead. The flames of that dream began to die over the decades. But still, I would dream, and in my dreams, I would see all those beautiful hills and the fields of the Steel Meadow Farm. I would meet my Savior there in my dreams. It was there in my dreams I would find peace and joy, walking in the tall fescue grass of the land I loved. I recall hearing a conversation with my mom and a crane salesman one day. Because my dad had put the crane in my Grandma Moore's name, to keep it from being seized by the IRS, it belonged to her. My grandpa could not sell it in the estate. The 30-ton Lorain crane was my favorite. It had a chrome straight stack coming off a big diesel engine. Out of all the crane operators my dad had, my mom said no one could change those gears like he did. She could always tell it was him, as she heard him coming through our small town. She knew by the changing of the gears in the transmission if it was him or not.

Anyway, as to the phone call, she was trying to sell the crane, and the salesman wanted to hear it run, and try it out. Daddy parked it, the day he got shot, along the main street of Cowpens in front of Mike's café. I decided to drive it home for her. I had never driven it before, but I had operated it on a few construction sites. And, I had watched my dad! I remember the sound of that exhaust pipe as it came to life. That diesel roared like the days of yesterday. It was as if the machine itself was grieving for my dad. That day, I got a small glimpse of what would be my destiny, as I climbed into the driver seat of that crane. I brought it through Cowpens and up Highway 110. I made it sound just like the ghost of my dad driving it. I brought it home and set it up for the man to try out. He bought it for $90,000. I was so thankful to be able to drive dad's Lorain crane, and hear it one more time. I started to feel "BIG."

Dad's truck in 1976

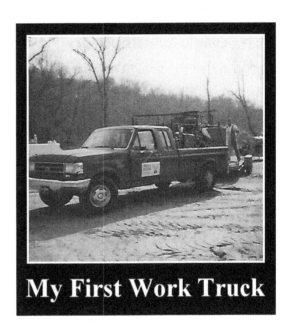

My First Work Truck

Mom bought a house in the city of Cowpens and began to spoil Clint and Clay. I married Angela Gilbert, and settled in a small two bedroom house in-between Cowpens and Converse, South Carolina.

The Lord blessed us with two beautiful girls born 15-months apart. Me, and my best friend, Angela, got busy with the business of life. I still had deep depression and began to drink heavily. I just couldn't deal with my life. I worked as a common laborer, picking up trash on construction sites. The same kind of construction sites my dad used to be in charge of. Now I was only qualified to pick up garbage. I did not have a welding certificate. And I did not have enough experience at this job, or that job, to be qualified. That was the most humbling experience to be responsible for raising a family on a laborer's pay. One day, as I was picking up trash in the parking lot of a nuclear power plant, under construction in North Carolina, I looked through the fence and saw a man welding on an earth mover bucket. I stood motionless. He looked just like my Dad! As I watched him weld from a distance, I began to be amazed at how he moved and walked just like daddy. There, standing with a five-gallon bucket and a poker stick for picking up debris, I almost called out to him! Then suddenly, I remembered again, he was indeed dead and gone. I never have been one to feel sorry for myself, but right then, right there, I did! I made the decision at that moment to do whatever it took to qualify myself to get inside the fence, and to move on to the construction sites of MY life!

I started taking classes at Spartanburg Technical College to get certified in welding.

I will never forget the first day of welding school. The instructor laughed at me and said, "HELL, I thought you knew how to weld. You should know how to weld. Your dad was one of the best welders in the state." I felt embarrassed and ashamed. I remember daddy watching me weld in a shop about one year before he died. He said, "Boy the things I can teach you!" But that never happened, and here I was at the welding school where my dad once taught, having to listen to this crap. I went into the welding rod and tool room to be alone. As I looked at all the different rods, and different torch tips, I smelled that familiar scent of the cowhide leather welding coats. I reflected on how talented, and smart my dad truly was. The task seemed intimidating, but I decided right then and there, that by God, I would be the best, too! And that I would learn it all!

Welding and I did not get along at all, at first. I just simply couldn't learn it, or get the hang of it, as fast as I wanted or needed to. I would ask for a lot of help and advice. I remember Mr. Conrad Allen telling me, "Hell son, you're not the only student I got." That statement hurt my feelings, but I did not let up! I was on a mission! My Heavenly Father, in his tender mercy, looked down from heaven, and saw a young man picking up trash during the day, and going to welding school at night, chasing his dad's ghost. The Almighty Creator of the universe, the greatest of them all, whispered to my mind, rod after rod, bead after bead. I don't really know how, but I began to understand. I began to see the hidden shadows of the molten metal, the slag, and the flux. My mind became clear. Looking back on it now, it was as if every weld I made, my dad was watching over my shoulder. My arms and back began to explode. I had strength like never before. I started to become a man. I became, during the course of two years with night after night experience, a slick welder. I became a good welder! I became confident.

"Plow it under."

After all of dad's things were liquidated, I later heard my mom talking to someone on the phone. She said, "Just plow it under. No, I don't want it; just plow it under the ground." I asked her what? She said, "Your dad's granite business sign. I just told your grandpa to bury it in the pasture." I remember the blood rushing through my mind and body! I said, "Oh, no, he won't!" You see, my dad brought his huge granite sign home when he lost his shop and laid it in the field beside the house. Everyone had forgotten about it. Engraved are the words, "WHY NOT THE BEST," on one side. On the other side it read, "STEVE'S WELDING SERVICE."

I took my half-ton pickup, a one-ton chain fall, an old engine stand, and left to retrieve his sign out of the field. My mom said just let it be buried. But I had plans for that sign. I worked eight hours that day lifting and cribbing to heave that piece of granite high enough to get it on my truck. It was not an easy feat. My uncle Joe Mathis must've felt sorry for me as he came to assist me later that evening. I remember how he cried like a baby the day we buried my daddy.

After the sign was loaded, I remember driving home feeling like the bed of the truck was dragging the ground. The front tires were barely touching the ground it was so heavy.

I tied the sign to a tree behind my little house by wrapping a nylon choker to it. That is the way I pulled it off the truck. The sign stayed in my backyard of our first house. It moved with us to our second house. It was always there; to some it looked like a tombstone from yesterday, but it looked like hope to me.

After I got the welding school completed, I began to travel around making good money, for the day. As I excelled in my professional life, I continued to slip in my spiritual life. I had taken a job at Hoechst-Celanese as a helper for seven dollars an hour. I did this, to get my foot in the door. As I worked there, and went to their training schools, I began to make better money. I certified as a welder, a precision millwright, and a precision millwright foreman, during my time there. I worked with the old men. I was determined to be the best helper they ever had. They in turn, taught me their secrets of the trade. They advised me on how grown men set each other up for failure, how they lie, and take credit for the accomplishments of others. I learned a lot about hydraulics, pneumatics, steam traps, coupling alignment, and mechanics. I learned, in order to learn, "You have to start at the bottom." "You have to ask questions." And, "You have to be quiet, so you don't have to ask as many questions!" Those old men, most of them dead now, taught me because I let them talk. I let them be the boss, and they showed me their tricks. I am thankful for them all. I am thankful to God who inspired me with the gift of learning. Who inspired me to listen first, talk later!

Joe and Linda Mathis

The Rebirth

I had been laid off from Hoechst, because of the economy and the NAFTA trade agreement, and I was working for Sanders Brothers. I had traveled around the country working power outages and shutdowns for paper mills, chemical plants, and nuclear power plants. Anyway, at this time I was working at home for Sanders Brothers as a welder and I heard some discussion about welding on a giant smokestack at Hoechst Celanese. The foreman said it was about 175 feet in the air, and they were looking for volunteers. I immediately volunteered for the job. It would be close to my house, and back out at the same Hoechst plant where I had worked for several years. It also had just a little to do with the fact that as a child, I had watched my dad make weld repairs high in the sky on those smokestacks at Hoechst Celanese. I can still see him in the man basket being lifted by those huge cranes from our house on the hill. Yes, our little house at Steel Meadow Farm, as it sat on the hill with the plant to the southeast in the distance. As it turned out, my job as I volunteered, would be the "inside man." My job would be to weld up a new section of stack that would be placed on top of, and higher than all the others. We used walkie-talkies to communicate with the crane and the transit operators. The pieces of the stack would go up 50 to 75 feet at a time. I would direct the crane that would fly the next section down over the top of me, as I was tied to the inside of each previous section. I was thrilled to see the stack go up, and to experience what my dad had so many years earlier.

Finally, it ascended higher than all the rest of the older smokestacks. When the last piece was to be set, the wind was blowing lightly out of the south. It was a beautiful day. It took me one half hour to climb up to the inside of the stack to get in position. Upon setting the last piece of stack high in the air, down over me, I began to fasten the Jack Bolts, and communicate with the transit team and crane operators as to the alignment of the last top piece. I had the thought several times to tie off high onto the top piece of stack, so that if I slipped on the inside ladder, I would not fall far, before my safety harness rope got taught. Each time I had that thought; I would get a sick feeling and hear the words in my mind, "No, don't do it." The last piece was difficult to align because the wind picked up. The Jack Bolts were tight as I tried to adjust them, and the crane cable pressure was tight. Then, all of a sudden, it happened. The force of the wind, crane cable pressure, and Jack bolts broke the top piece loose. As it broke free it took off like a rocket! It bounced up about 25 feet into the air above me, and it came crashing down again onto the existing stack. The force of the impact knocked me loose from the inside ladder, and had me dangling from my safety rope on the inside, bouncing around like a Mexican jumping bean. It knocked my walkie-talkie loose. The crane operator jumped out of the crane the moment it happened. He thought the crane would turn over. Down on the ground people were running everywhere, as time after time, the last section would bounce up and down crashing against the existing stack. The crashing sounds were deafening inside the stack. The vibrations of the impacts were enough to convince me that the whole stack was falling.

Men were on the ground assembling a rescue team to climb up the stack to find me. Finally, I got my hand back on the walkie-talkie. The call was, "Are you still alive?" "Yes," I responded, "I reckon so." If I had tied off to the top piece, I would have been jerked out of the stack when the top piece broke free. There would have been no way to survive the impact of the crashing stack or the 175 foot fall that would have resulted with my harness being cut in two, if, I managed to miss the colliding pieces of the stack. I knew my life had been spared by God. I realized in a very profound way that I had lost my relationship with Him, and that I had become inactive in the LDS church. I felt very guilty. I thought about the fact that had my life ended that day, who would have told my wife of the Plan of Salvation, the Restoration of the gospel, or of *The Book of Mormon*. I realized that if I didn't tell my wife and kids about the gospel, and my testimony of it, then I really couldn't say that I loved them. One thing was for sure, I knew that I loved them, with all my heart. I did not know it at the time, but God had already put a plan into motion to bring the gospel back to us. I just knew I had to change. I had to save my marriage, rebuild my relationship with God, and my wife.

The plan God put in motion came a few nights later, as I sat in the den of our second home located at Robin Court. The situation was tense as usual between me and Angela. We were so stressed out from the pressures of life with little kids. There came a knock on our door. Three men in trench coats stood outside our door at the carport. The weather was cold, rainy, and foul. At first, I thought they were insurance salesman. And as I was in a bad mood, I got up to answer the door to immediately run them off. When I opened the door, I recognized them as Mormon missionaries. They had looked up our new address and found me after 10 years of inactivity. As they introduced themselves, the Spirit of the Lord was overwhelming. I had not felt His Spirit in such a very long time. The Holy Spirit I felt so long ago, so very long ago, His Spirit of peace, of love so complete, strong, and pure. It was like a fire. I could not welcome them into my house fast enough. They were our messengers.

Every Boy's Dream

I guess to go back a few years to explain the way me and my wife came to be together, will take you back to the seventh grade at Cowpens Jr. High School. I had been sent to reform school at the middle of fifth grade. I got sent to Tabernacle Baptist Christian Academy. It was for grades one through twelve. I had a preacher for a teacher; Preacher Hembree. He would grit his teeth together and beat us with a yardstick if we got out of control; which we did, a lot. We had to memorize a scripture per week, and to be honest, I did not mind that at all, because I had an unexplainable curiosity about the Bible. And it wasn't like my mother did not take us boys to church.

At the reform school I discovered I could box. One day Preacher Hembree decided he would let us put the gloves on. I whipped everyone in my class. I enjoyed beating people with my fist. I guess I inherited that from my father and my grandpa. Anyhow, at the start of the seventh grade my father convinced School District 3 to let me come back to school, and with that I busted into the Cowpens Junior High Red Raider scene with my white Converse All-Stars, and red tag Levis. Cooler than cool, was I! Or at least I thought so.

I will never forget the first time I saw Angela Gilbert. Man-Oh-Man, she was pretty! She was the green eyed, brown haired, gal who looked like she had been molded into her jeans. She had a mouth-full of braces, and the absolute, most beautiful feet I had ever seen. She wore Bass sandals, wore red toenail polish, pigtails, lip gloss, and her mouth was always full of bubblegum. Boy, her lips sure did shine as she smiled. And, she had the ability to smile with her eyes, too. She was surely any young boy's dream. I started to think about how to make her mine. The first time I spoke to her in science class, she looked at me and said, "You can forget it!" I thought, "How rude." But, I also thought, "We will see about that!" For the rest of the school year I kept a sharp lookout for that sharp looking honey pie. Whenever I saw her, I made sure I was acting a fool, or just simply staring at her to catch her eye. Older boys liked her. I wanted to beat the fool out of every one of them!

At the start of the eighth grade we were assigned the same algebra class. I was so thrilled to see her in my class that first day. I knew this would be one of the places that I might just get to impress her. The first day, the mean old teacher, Mrs. McGowan, well into her 60s, called my name. She pointed her finger at me from across the desk and said, "I know you. I taught your dad! You ain't gonna pick up where he left off!" The whole class erupted in laughter. I was thankful on the inside for her compliment! I would show out, crack jokes, act as stupid as it took to get Angela's attention. I ended up sitting across from her. The day came when I found a reason to pass her a note, a little joke here and there. Then, finally, a little conversation, like, "Do you have another piece of gum?" Or, "Do you want a Jolly Rancher?" She loved watermelon flavored Jolly Ranchers. Her lips and tongue looked so great every day. I fantasized about kissing her. I wanted her bad…

I had her friend Teresa Brigman, and others telling her that I liked her. I had them trying to convince her to like me. Finally, the day came when I passed a note that said, "Will you go with me?" The note came back, and the answer was yes! Over the years from the eighth grade through the twelfth Angela and I would go together and break up numerous times. I had a lot of issues going on at home with mom and dad. Also, I played a lot of sports and football. I wanted to be a professional football player; a quarterback. Angela was always on the cheerleading team, and always the most beautiful. I met her in the seventh grade, and as we both grew up through school, I began to realize how beautiful she was on the inside. She was a gem, one of the nicest people you would ever want to meet. She was a friend to everyone, yet she seemed oblivious to her beauty. She loved to laugh, especially at me. We would talk on the phone for hours. We would write letters, but sometimes I would be too scared to talk to her at school. I would think about, and stress over, and plan what I would wear each day to school to look perfect for her.

We kissed for the first time at the end of the eighth grade. I had never kissed a girl before! We were on a field trip for school, I'm pretty sure it was at the Rose Hill plantation house. We set beside each other. It was apparent, that as she smiled and blew chewing gum bubbles that she wanted to kiss me. I knew she knew what to do because I had seen her kiss another boyfriend, before, in the seventh grade. I knew I had one shot at it, and if it wasn't good, she would be gone. My heart was pounding, and I thought I would die. I knew for sure that I did not know what to do, and how to kiss a girl. So, I thought to myself, "I'll just simply do what she does." I leaned in, she as well. Our lips met, and we kissed. She opened her mouth slowly and passionately. So, I did the same, and *Oh my Granny Goodness*! There is not a stick of dynamite that ever exploded like my little heart did that day. It was a day that will never be forgotten. I am thankful that somehow, I had the common sense to let her lead me, and show me how to kiss. If I had tried to be a know-it-all cowboy, I am sure that kiss would have been a two for one; in other words, the first and the last. I always enjoyed our talks, our walks, and the times we were able to spend together. I knew deep inside that she would be a good member of the church. I knew she was pure of heart. I just really did not know if we could make it work for a lifetime. She was a fiery little girl. She was very passionate about being fair and seeing justice in any situation. She would fight you if you made her mad. She seemed somehow to have the ability to subdue the devil in me. She seemed to always be up to the task. I was happy and at peace with her. She took my mind completely off of the problems at home, and the worry of where daddy was, and what he was doing, etc.

I am so thankful that Angela and I found each other. I am glad we were together at such a young age. I am eternally grateful that God answered my prayers on that same day, when I heard the words, "Behold thy family." I remember my dad saying one time to me, while I was acting stupid, and had Angela mad at me, he said, "Son are you a fool?" He knew she was a keeper.

Diamond in the Moonlight

After dad died, I threw a fit for a Harley Davidson motorcycle. So, mom bought it for me. I was an 18-year-old teenager with a drinking problem. How she thought I was competent to ride a motorcycle is beyond me. But, I didn't have any problem riding Angela around on my bike.

It was a hot summer night when I decided to pop the question. We were riding that night alongside a northbound freight train on Highway 29. The Carolina moon was full, and the stars were shining bright. My Harley was roaring through the night air. I reached into my side jacket pocket and pulled out a little diamond ring that I had bought for her. As I tried to take her hand, she was hesitant about turning my waist loose. Finally, she let go and I tried to place that ring on her finger. I knew that if I dropped it, I would not tell her what it was. That would be my sign that it wasn't meant to be.

As fate would have it. I didn't! She screamed and yelled with joy as we rode down the highway. "Are you sure?" she asked. "Hell, Yes!" was my response. I rode her around that night making her hold her hand up to see the ring in the moonlight. She was, and still is, my diamond in the moonlight. There will never be another to take her place. We have been together twenty-five years. And, as I sit along the Ocean Lakes, at Surfside Beach, to write this book, I can say that I'm so grateful to my wife, my eighth grade sweetheart, as she sits here now. She is still my diamond in the moonlight. The Lord made it pretty obvious. We went to the same daycare, same kindergarten, she lived and slept in the same room as my mother did growing up, and we did not know these amazing details until after we were married. When dad and I went to find a wife, they had lived at the same address, and we walked the same porch steps merely eighteen years apart. Kinda crazy, huh?

Back to the Missionaries

June 24, 2012 Hilton Head, South Carolina

I invited the missionaries inside, and they were happy to come into our home. Again, immediately the Spirit of the Lord entered our home. They informed us that we were in the Spartanburg 1st ward now. Brother Brian Ruppe was one of the members who came over that day. I remember when I was a young boy and attended church at Gaffney, that Brian was inactive and driving his mother crazy. Now, he was all cleaned up and serving the Lord. He was an amazing example of what faith, prayer, and repentance can do to, and for, a man. Brian suggested that he could invite a young couple he knew from the Spartanburg first ward to come over and meet us. We agreed, and so the next couple of days brought Troy and Elizabeth Williams, and more missionaries to our home. Troy was from the Idaho Rocky Mountains. He had served a mission for the church in North Carolina. While at Rick's College, Troy met and fell in love with Elizabeth Chapman, who was from Spartanburg, South Carolina. She was a girl that I had attended seminary with years ago. Troy and Elizabeth had great personalities and a great love for the gospel. A friendship was formed with them immediately and continued for years. Troy and I have bow hunted often for white tailed deer, and elk. I am thankful for his friendship and testimony.

The missionaries began to teach my wife, and she was in shock, of how much I knew and believed about the Bible, the gospel, *The Book of Mormon*, and the first vision and restoration of the gospel. She began to see me in a different light, herself in a different light, our marriage in a different light, but most especially, the Savior of the world, even Jesus Christ, the Son of Almighty God, in a very different light.

Satan tried his best to sabotage her conversion, but the Spirit of the Lord was too overpowering. During the missionary visits and discussions, it was undeniable to her that she was hearing the truth.

Our marriage was resurrected by the healing power of Jesus Christ. We were on our way to a life of happiness. My wife was so beautiful the day she was baptized. I am thankful for Elder Nielson who relied on the Holy Ghost to teach her. One year later we were sealed in the Washington, D.C. Temple for time and all eternity. It was during this time of her conversion that I decided to repent and come back into active membership of the church.

It was a kind and wise Bishop Mather who helped me realize how I punished myself for many years, holding on to grief and pain that I had no control over. He helped me see that Jesus Christ had already suffered, bled, and died that I might live and have life more abundantly. I was very happy to be active again in the church. We had our third baby during this time, another girl! Her name is Connor. So, we have Casey, Catelyn, and Connor. Casey continues to be a very beautiful well-rounded girl who loves to be in charge. She seemed to be okay. But Catelyn was another story. We knew early on that she had developmental problems. The doctor said she was mentally impaired. We were so devastated by this, and it drove Angela over the edge mentally as well. She carried her to all kinds of doctors, and genetic research centers, trying to figure out a syndrome or a cure. But nothing to date has ever been derived as to Catelyn's special needs. She could read on a college level, but was very limited in math and social skills. She is 24-years-old now and still is at home with us. We take it day by day, and pray that God will bless her to live a happy, long life.

Connor was four months old when we went together as a family to be sealed for time and all eternity as husband and wife, and as a family. We decided to go to the Washington, D.C. Temple. Troy and Elizabeth, their son Dusty, and grandma, came with us. I will never forget the day. Angela was disgusted with her hair, and threw the hairbrush into the motel's sink in front of the mirror. I thought she looked beautiful, but somehow, she just couldn't make herself pretty enough for our special day. I will never forget that beautiful day as she gripped my hand, ever so tightly, as we entered in the temple. I knew she wanted us to be "forever," just as much as I did!

The experience of our marriage in the temple is too sacred to share, but as we knelt at the sacred altar, our little children joining us, the Spirit was overwhelming, as to the glimpses, and promises of what eternity will be and will hold for us, if we are faithful. An undeniable witness of truth is based 100% on the pure love of Christ, the miracle of the atonement, and of God's overwhelming love for His children. It is a blessing that I can only hope to live for. My only desire is to be in the presence of God with my loved ones near me. I pray for strength, to hold faithful to the promises and covenants that we made at that Holy place, and that Holy time, on that Holy day.

Day of Preparation

After our marriage for time and all eternity, Angela and I began to come together in a way like we had never been before. We had goals, we had a plan, and we had each other. I began to understand her, to feel her, and to realize more of everything she needed. We made plans to receive our patriarchal blessings. Our individual blessings revealed more of our Heavenly Father's plan for us. It warned us of things to come. Our blessings gave us hope that our lives would be beautiful if we held on to the gospel truths. I began to grow spiritually and physically. After two more years we became pregnant with our fourth child. It only lived several months in her womb. It was a very sad time for us to lose this child. But, our faith kept us right on track spiritually. After she had a DNC, I gave her a nice big diamond ring in the recovery room. I wanted it to be a symbol of our family, what we had lost, and of our love being eternal. I got the ring as payment for the fabrication and installation of handrails for the Geiss and Sons Hilton Head Island jewelry store. But, wait, let me go back and tell you how I ended up in business for myself.

Side Rails/Handicap Ramp

Geiss and Sons Hilton Head Island

SWS
July 14, 2013 Fripp Island, South Carolina

As a young boy I idolized my dad and his welding truck. I listened intensely every day about sundown for the sound of the blue Ford truck with the steel welding bed, and the welding machine mounted on the back, to come down our driveway. Daddy didn't have to tell me he worked hard. It was evident by the way he moved at the end of the day. Soaked in sweat or frozen nearly to death, he was my inspiration. He taught me the very basics of welding, the art of working with fire and metal. I had always dreamed of working with him. I knew it was my destiny to be an SWS Ironworker and Welder. As a kid I dreamed of walking the iron in the sky, of building skyscrapers, and big industrial buildings. But, how could I make it happen now? Where do I begin? When do I start?

Over the years I had accomplished a great deal as a welder. I could work anywhere I wanted to. Because of going back on site for the Hoechst Fibers smokestack job, I got to see my old friend; my Godfather, Rufus Whelchel. He wasn't really my Godfather; it is just a name he took for himself. He started out welding along with my dad back when they were just young folks and first getting started. He was now a supervisor of the (Staple A) dungeon bottom maintenance shop. He offered me a chance to come back and work for Fluor Daniel Inc. at that site. I had cut my teeth there as a young, inexperienced, desperate kid. I learned so much from those outstanding craftsmen. I had so much respect for Rufus, he was my godfather, my first godfather that is; I'll explain all this later. I took the job and began to flourish. I was dial indicating pump shafts and welding every day. Then I heard, and read in the news, that General Electric was hiring at the Gas Turbine plant in Greenville, South Carolina. My good friend Steve Faltermeier, from my high school years, was working there. I knew it was one of the highest paying jobs in South Carolina and offered excellent benefits. A total of 5000 people applied the day of the job fair in Greenville. I remember that long, long, line. I was one of only a couple hundred chosen to qualify for the training program at Greenville Technical College. The first phase was an academic assessment of reading, writing, and math skills. There was an aptitude test as well as a drug test that had to be passed. I thank God for preparing me for both. After completing the specialty training schools, I had to begin the welding school at night. I had to pass several carbon and a stainless pipe tests or I could not be hired on a GE. There were unfortunately men who could not pass these welding tests. The tests were x-ray tests, where the welds would be x-rayed, and the tiniest flaw detected. I can remember praying to God with each test, that He would correct my mistakes, if any, in each weld. Those were very sincere, private, and desperate moments between the Lord and me. I passed each test to gain a job at GE! I never failed an x-ray test the whole time I worked there. The Lord was faithful, and perfect in looking after my interest, and blessing my arm and hand to become a master welder.

I began working at GE as a wild-eyed young man who had just won the lottery of sorts. Now I could make the money I needed to give our family a good life. I can say that leaving the Hoechst Fibers basement shop was no easy thing for me. I remember overhearing my boss Rufus brag one day to someone else, how I had shown him eight zeros on my dial indicators. This means I had aligned the couplings perfectly. I also overheard him bragging that I was only one of fifty to actually make it into GE out of 5000 applicants. He never gave me a lot of praise. Those kind, overheard compliments were sacred to me. I knew he wouldn't give them unless he truly believed I had accomplished something special.

Rufus Whelchel

Rufus Whelchel came from German descendants. He had brothers; Tom, Mose, Richard, and Furman. They had a wonderful mother, Lillian. Their dad, Rhett, was called the sheriff because he kept those boys in line. One day, as a small child, I remember seeing the old man sheriff, walking across the field. He was using a walking cane, and was not detected by the Whelchel boys, as they were busy butchering a cow. The Whelchels were farmers and butchers. They were also extremely on the wild side. As the group of boys (men), were supposedly butchering the cow, they were telling dirty jokes, spitting tobacco, and drinking moonshine whiskey. I was very young, and I was amazed at the sight of seeing a cow butchered. My dad was among the crowd of men standing there. I noticed some men grow silent, and soon began to step away looking like they were searching for something on the ground. This, as the old man sheriff came within steps of his Whelchel boys. I never knew what was coming next, I had never seen an old man in his 70s move so fast. Mose and two or three brothers never saw their dad coming. They continue to cuss, spit tobacco, and guzzle down whiskey. Mose was the youngest, he was cutting the skin off the cow's belly with a buck knife when the old oak walking cane came crashing across his neck. Whaaap! Mose screamed in agony, as in the surprise of the attack, he had drug the knife down and across his arm cutting himself. "God! Daddy, look what you…" Crack! The cane came across his head! The old man was swinging his cane and quoting the Bible. I never saw grown men scatter so fast from the righteous indignation of an angry father. It was one of the most shocking things I ever saw in my life.

Rufus Whelchel was, and still is to this day, a genius of common sense and mechanical ingenuity. He always displayed a brilliant mind in my mechanical workplace. He and his family were blessed with intelligence from on High. All the engineers consulted with him for the tough problems. So, I am glad that when my dad died, and I found myself picking up trash on construction sites as a day laborer, that Rufus remembered his friendship with my dad and helped me get a job where I could learn so much. He gave me a key. I took that key and entered into my profession.

Today I still see Rufus. He is retired and raises cows, corn, watermelons, and everything else you would like to grow in a garden. He always has a project going on, to improve some farm implement or process. Rufus spends the summer with his grandson who comes up from Texas. The 10-year-old grandson who Rufus calls "Dude," is living the golden days of the adventure. As part of my story I want to give credit to the people who helped me along my way.

"Thank you, Rufus." You were there when I needed you.
I am glad to still have you as a trusted friend.

Rufus Whelchel

Working at GE

As I began to work the third shift at GE, I began to pick it up and excel in my department (Nozzles). We welded high alloy inserts into the arrangements, and the fuel nozzles of the gas turbines. It was tedious, painstaking welding. The high alloys were always prone to cracks. The Quality Control Technicians were ever so careful to try and detect welding flaws. We spent the night welding, then we would penetrant dye test the welds. Then we would have to get a QC to sign off our welds before removing the dye and developer of each nozzle piece. GE was like no other place I had seen. If you wanted to work, by all means, you could. If you did not want to work, you did not have to! A lot of folks just walked around and talked most of the night. It was funny stories, hunting stories in the winter, fishing stories in the summer, football commentary, baseball, basketball, racing, anything to keep grown men and women arguing and laughing to pass the time. It was a shocking contrast to the working environment where I had come from. Inside Hoechst Fibers it was extremely hot, steamy, physically demanding, and dangerous. Up on the iron as an ironworker it was so physically abusive to your body. Now, at GE, it was air-conditioned and heated. It was massive and huge, with thousands of people running around everywhere making the most sophisticated machinery, and the most expensive gas turbines in the world. It was always hurry up and wait. We had all new tools and a new pair of welding gloves every night, if you wanted. Work and be serious, or simply goof off, the choice was yours.

I was scared of all the idleness and waste. I feared the layoffs. I had seen them before in other places I worked because of the NAFTA trade agreement. "Never here at GE!" was the response I was told. "This is the big-time, son" is what I constantly heard. I wondered if it was really true. Could this company have this much inefficiency and still be successful? I knew in my heart that a company is only as good as the leadership and employee's attitudes. Time would tell the truth. But for now, I had the biggest test to deal with, the anti-Mormons. I did not recognize it when I went to work at GE at least not at first, but soon I began to feel the disdain and disgust when I told my workmates that I was a Latter Day Saint. Not all were stand-offish. There were a few who didn't care. There were some who were actually interested in my religion. Donna, a friend on my crew, actually attended church with me on a few occasions. But, for the most part everyone who heard I was a Mormon wanted to save my soul from Hell's fire!

It has always amazed me how I found the story of the first vision of Joseph Smith to be so true and beautiful, and how it can cause so many others to be so angry and upset when they hear it. I guess it is, as Nephi wrote of this, while under the guidance of the Holy Ghost, when he said there would be some who would receive the truth with gladness, while others would be sorrowful and angry because of the gospel. At GE I ran into countless people affiliated with Bob Jones University. It is a seminary Bible college where all young men who aspire to be Baptist preachers seem to find themselves enrolled. I knew of all the hostility and anger of anti-Mormons. I had seen them protest the opening of the Atlanta temple. It seemed to me that a dark force of opposition always accompanied them. Such was the case as I encountered them at GE. They would always come up smiling initially. They would then begin to challenge me in my beliefs with things like, "I heard you Mormons believe in so-and-so, or is it true y'all worship Joseph Smith?" I would be infuriated and embarrassed a lot, but I could always withstand them with my testimony and my knowledge of the scriptures. The more they realized that I knew the Holy Bible, the more determined to prove me wrong they were. I saw people staring at me at times, other times two and three were gathered together in my vicinity, and eventually after a discussion, they would approach me. I was very happy of my knowledge of the restoration of the gospel. I was sure of my witness of the boy prophet, Joseph Smith Jr. I was sure that God had revealed the truthfulness of *The Book of Mormon* to me. I waited on the Lord each time before I would speak. I listened to my heart. I would be prompted as to what to say, and how to say the things the Lord put on my heart.

I gave *The Book of Mormon* to my coworkers who would receive one. I would notice, soon after someone talked to me, and showed interest in my church or would take *The Book of Mormon*; it wouldn't be long before Satan would get his message to them by way of anti-Mormon literature. It was passed out continually by these fine men of God at GE, who were convinced I was of the devil, and deceived.

I had one day given a book to a man named Chip. He and I went through the GE special schools together. One day in a meeting, my coworker Chip came up to me in front of everyone and said, "I can't find anything about Jesus in this book! I read it, I don't get it, here take it back." Because he did this in front of everyone, I was humiliated. I could feel my face grow red. I was confounded, and I was hurt inside. Everyone was looking at me as he walked away. Then I heard very clearly, the Holy Ghost whisper to me. The words that he put into my mind, and that came out of my mouth were, "You did not read it! Did you?" Chip turned around and looked down at the ground. He said, "No! My wife will not let me bring that book in our house. I kept it outside in the truck!" At that moment everyone in the room started laughing at Chip! They said, "Oh, so your wife is in charge! Ha, ha, ha, ha, ha!" As the laughter rang out, the attention immediately shifted away from me and on to Chip. I stood there amazed as I realized the Lord would not have me embarrassed, and ridiculed, for spreading the gospel of Jesus Christ. I realized in depth, at that moment, that the gift of the Holy Ghost is real, and that he can influence us, rescue us, inspire us, comfort us, and in fact does these things if we allow it to happen within our soul.

I got handed a lot of anti-Mormon literature. I took it home. I studied it. I felt the dark, depressing feelings associated with it. My blood boiled at its horrible lies, of its half-truths, and all the things taken out of context. It validated the undeniable fact that Joseph Smith's name would be as the angel Moroni proclaimed, "Had for both good and evil," in the world. Nevertheless, I had the burning Spirit of the Great Jehovah within my heart. I knew of the truth.

The anti-Mormons had mostly given up on me after a couple of years. They had given an old machinist by the name of Ron, the chance to be their leader, their champion. About every other night, or two, Ron would stop by my welding booth, to politely preach me into Hell. I would thank him kindly and give him a few scriptures along the way. One night he brought a couple of young boys with him and the discussion became bitter, as to whether Mormons were Christians or not. I could see the wrath of bitterness and gall in Ron's eyes as he informed me, once again, how I was not truly SAVED, and if I died, I would go straight to Hell. As I started to lose my temper, the inspiration came. I simply told Ron and his associates to look at the big mechanical clock hanging in the bay beyond us. I asked him if he could see the second hand ticking. He replied yes. I looked him in the eye and said, "I believe in Jesus Christ! I know Him, and He knows me by name! He is my Lord, and my mighty King! When he hung on the cross at Calvary and said, "It is finished, Father I commend my spirit unto thee," that is when Jesus Christ saved us all! And, now Ron, right this very second, I would not trade one more second on that clock for what I know to be true! I wouldn't want to live another second without my knowledge of the truthfulness of the gospel of Jesus Christ, and my membership in His true church!" Ron and his company walked away without speaking another word, and they never, ever, came back!

Steve studying plans.

Teaching at Spartanburg Technical College

One day, I heard Spartanburg Technical College was looking for a welding instructor, for the second shift. I went out to the college and met a black man by the name of William Reeder. He has since died of cancer. Mr. Reeder began to look at my resume. He was having some insubordination issues with some of his instructors, who were most likely wanting his job when he retired. He asked me to tell him why he should hire me? I told him without hesitation, "Because I am a Christian, and an honest man." He immediately stretched out his hand and a true friendship was born. He said I was the only one who had mentioned having faith. The job was mine. I looked into my mirror of life, and I felt very humble to once again be at Spartanburg Tech. The place that I spent inside a welding booth learning to watch the fire and molten steel. I spent many hours in constant prayer and struggle in these walls as a young man. Now, I could inspire other young men. I could teach them what I had learned through trial and error. I wondered what my dad would think. I had become an instructor at Spartanburg Technical College just like he did! How would this affect my life? It seemed a little scary that my life seemed to still be following, or at least attached to his. I knew that I should be careful of this omen. I was determined to follow my Heavenly Father's lead. I was driven to be someone my wife could be proud of.

My days of teaching welding were very rewarding. I saw the ones who gave up. I saw the ones who had the gift. I taught the ones who struggled and were diamonds in the rough. It does my heart good to see them from time to time. It is an incredible feeling to help someone learn and achieve something. My son Cross has just turned 14 now. I'm excited to get a chance to teach him to weld, and to cut with a torch. My two brothers Clint and Clay came to Spartanburg Technical College while I was teaching there. They both have experience in the welding field but more on that later.

So, by now I was staying busy and enjoying my family. Everything seemed to be working out just fine as we were expecting another child. I could not have ever imagined that my life was heading for a head on collision with fate. And, because of this, my life would be turned upside down, and I would be sent in an entirely different direction.

A Steve's Welding Service crane lifts a pre-cast panel into place during construction of the entrance into Sears' ladies' ready-to-wear departments. In 1975, Steve's Welding Service erected almost 100,000 tons of steel in over 5 million square feet of building construction in the southeast. The same technique has been used in dozens of larger and smaller buildings for business and industry all over the Spartanburg area.

By Anne H. Foster

IT ALL STARTED AT TEC

I just wanted what a lot of people want....a better life for my family and for myself. I was about to have to go to another state to take a welding course in 1964 when Everett Clarkson (a member of the Board of Commissioners at Spartanburg TEC) suggested to my mother that I go out to Spartanburg TEC and take their welding course."

"In just a few short months, I had a skill that people were looking for in a prospective employee. Now I could do the welding that people were needing. I had started on the way to that better life I wanted."

That's how Steve Mathis, a Spartanburg TEC graduate, feels about the education he received at Spartanburg Technical College. He is very reticent to use the word "success" in describing his present business but he is not at all reluctant to describe the vital part Spartanburg TEC had played in his life. In fact, he says that "TEC is the only place that could have made it possible to do what I'm doing now."

Steve's Welding and Steel Erecting Service is headquartered in his hometown of Cowpens, S.C., a few miles east of Spartanburg TEC. From his offices come the bids that are responsible for the structural steel that supports such outstanding projects as the new Westgate Mall in Spartanburg (875,000 sq. ft. enclosed) and a one million square foot mall in Kingsport, Tenn., two of Arlen Shopping Centers Company's newest retailing centers. Steve also submitted the accepted bids for the structural steel for Westgate Village

(Winn Dixie, Roses and Eckerds) and for the K-Mart and A&P Stores on the corners near the Westgate Mall at the intersection of I-26 and U.S.29, west of Spartanburg.

The list of successful bids in recent years by Steve's Welding and Steel Erecting Service goes on to include the First Federal Savings and Loan Association on East Main in Spartanburg, the Boiling Springs Middle School, an addition to Metromont Materials on I-85, a new plant for Harley Bag Corp. (a box plant at Whitestone), the G.E. Home Appliance Plant at Asheboro, N.C., the 3-M Plant at Donaldson Center, Greenville, the new garage at the Michelin Test Track in Laurens and many more smaller business and industrial buildings.

The new seven-story University Medical Service Building in Charleston presented a challenge to Steve Mathis that he eagerly accepted and marked a milestone for his structural steel business.

At present, he is submitting bids on jobs in Florida and other neighboring states. He finds it all still a little hard to believe.

"When I was making $1.75 per hour in 1964," he says, "I heard that welders were getting $3.60 per hour. That's when I went to Spartanburg TEC to learn to weld. Mr. Newton took me in hand and saw to it that I learned to weld. In fact, when he saw how determined I was to learn welding, he suggested that I go to TEC five nights per week instead of the

14   impact

usual three nights for that course."

"Then Mr. Newton offered that extra assistance that so many TEC instructors are willing to do for their students. He helped me to find some weekend welding jobs. I had no welding machine so I rented one. I had to park it in my front yard. It didn't look so good but it helped bring me in some additional work. I was certified about that time and from there it was a short step to "pipe work." But when I bid on pipe work for construction, I was frequently told "No, we already have the contractor for that....What we need is somebody to put up steel."

"So I decided that sounded pretty good and I took on some modest jobs doing the steel work. Our first job was the Union (S.C.) Vocational High School. I had never bid on a steel job so after talking with the people at Union, I pulled onto the shoulder of the road and figured out how to handle it. I had to rent a crane because I had no adequate equipment to handle steel. Then I had to pull together a crew from a lot of places. Only then could we get to work."

To lift a pre-cast concrete panel weighing 8 tons or more into its proper place on the Harley Box Plant wall require cranes and properly placed hooks. Steve Mathis, (below right), is working with Donald Harris, one of the 25 to 35 men in Steve's crew at all times.

In one day, Steve's crew can set these 8 x 23' pre-cast panels into place to put up a 200 linear foot wall.

From that rented welding machine and crane, Steve's Welding and Steel Erecting Service has grown in just a few years to include four cranes, two tractors, six trailers, a yardlift and eleven welding machines (ranging from the 200 amp gasoline driven models to the new 600 amp semi-automatic wire welders) or well over a half-million dollars worth of equipment.

Steve had a fulltime job in an industry (just in case it didn't work out with the structural steel business). And one Monday something happened that changed his life. His steel crew failed to show up on the construction site and Steve had to quit his plant job. His superintendent hated to lose him but when Steve explained why, he left with the good wishes of his bosses.

How does Steve Mathis feel? "Very, very lucky," he says. A lot of men in my TEC classes have worked harder than I've had to, but I've been very lucky to be in some of the right places at some of the right times and it's working out pretty good for us right now."

"I'm also lucky to have such good and loyal men in my crew. Some have been with me since there were just two and then three of us. Those were the days of the rented crane and rented space in an old cotton gin to store our tools."

"I'm lucky in lots of ways and one of the best pieces of luck was finding out about technical education. TEC is the only place that could have made it possible for us to learn these skills that are in such great demand."

"When I was certified in welding at TEC about 9 years ago, I had no idea that what I had learned would give me the flexibility to go from welding to structural steel to pre-cast concrete to meet the demands in construction. The courses at TEC are not a one way street but more like a network of highways and it's up to each student to pick the routes they want to follow, using the skills they've learned."

"Some people might think it sounds funny but for a man like me who was only making $1.75 per hour, TEC gave me such a new start that it was a little like being born again. Spartanburg TEC taught me a marketable skill that makes me more valuable to my community and to myself and that skill is now helping me to do what I started out to do....earn a better life for my family. What do I think of TEC? I think it's great."

Steve Mathis is still part of Spartanburg TEC. Welding Department Head Conrad Allen (also a graduate of Spartanburg TEC) asked Steve to serve on the Advisory Committee for Welding. Because of his experience both as a student and as a business man, Steve is able to make many valuable contributions to Spartanburg TEC's Welding Department.

He feels very strongly about the help he recieved by attending Spartanburg TEC and he urges young people to investigate what Spartanburg TEC has for them. As he says, "Everyone wants to live the better life and learning a skill at TEC is a smart way to start."

And that's pretty good advice from a man who knows what he's talking about.

Anne H. Foster is Community Relations Coordinator at Spartanburg TEC.

Collision with Fate

At this point in my life I was working at GE on the third shift, teaching welding at Spartanburg technical College on the second shift, and enjoying my life just as things were. One winter day it began to sleet. Our roof got iced over and began to leak in a spot over our dining room. Angela and I placed a bucket or two in the various spots to catch the water, as it dripped through the ceiling. I had just been paid that night and wanted to take my paycheck to the bank, pick up some baby food, and milk at the store. Angela had a burgundy Honda Civic that was a front wheel drive, and I felt it would be fine in the icy conditions. I left our home and I drove about 5 miles from home on Cannons Campground Road. I was at the foot of the river approaching the old iron bridge when I spotted a car coming fast down the hill from the opposite direction toward me. As it approached the bridge, the car lost control. It began to pinball, bounce back and forth from one side of the bridge to the other. I knew the situation was dangerous, and I knew I had to try and avoid a collision, but I could have never been prepared for what was to happen next. I was going about 45 miles an hour when I began to break for the bridge and its icy surface. I guess the giant green Pontiac Catalina was traveling close to 60 miles an hour when it lost control. At the last second, I braced onto the steering wheel as tight as I could and thought that perhaps I could miss it. The last time the big car struck the left side of the bridge, it came like a slingshot right in front of my little Honda. I will never forget that horrible impact. My chest slammed into the steering wheel with great force. I never had experienced anything like it on the football field, or anywhere else. Instantly I felt its ferocious impact. It was so deep, so horrid. My torso hit the steering wheel so hard it bent the steering column in toward the middle of the car. All I could see was smoke, twisted medal, and broken glass. I could see the bloody faces of the two black women in front of me, dazed and confused in their car. I remember it felt like my whole body was humming. It felt like an elephant was standing on my chest. Suddenly, I realized I couldn't breathe. I began to panic, and something instinctively told me that I had to get out of the car and try to stand up, or I was going to die. It felt like a telephone pole had been rammed through my chest. I finally managed to get the seatbelt, which did not work, loose and unlatched. I pushed the door open and managed to stand up. I leaned back against the car in an effort to be able to breathe. It was excruciating to do so. The humming and ringing in my ears continued. Within moments another car came up to the scene. It was a high school friend of mine named Sammy Floyd. He was looking so shocked and wide-eyed. He said, "I've called 911, just be calm." I said, "Sammy, I don't feel good, tell them to hurry." Then the panic and terror set into my soul. My heart was humming and I could not seem to breathe. I thought of how unprepared I was for this moment! I had no forewarning, no clue that this was going to happen. It was all that I could do to absorb that impact. I thought of my wife at home, pregnant with our fourth child, catching water from our leaking, ice covered roof. I began to pray to God for mercy and relief. And then it happened…

Just as defining as the promptings of the Holy Ghost had been in my life, I could hear the words coming into my mind, "He is not here! He is not listening! Do you really believe in God?" A feeling of great despair accompanied those words. I was made very aware at that moment, I believe, by the Lord, that Satan was testing my faith. It's very hard to explain, but I truly feel that a battle for my life, and my soul, took place on that icy road that fateful day. I continued to call upon the name of my Lord Jesus! I thought of how my wife looked across the altar from me as her and our children were sealed for time and all eternity on that beautiful sunny day in Washington, D.C. I thought about how she would have to push this new baby into the world without me. I decided with God's help, I would breathe, with God's help I would live!

Hope came with the sound of sirens and the ambulance. Although I have since forgotten the name of the paramedic who attended to my immediate needs, I have not forgotten his face or his confidence in his ability. He said to me, "Don't worry

Mr. Mathis. I ain't lost one yet; I'm not losing you today. Here comes a big stick, I got to get a lifeline." As that young man pierced my flesh with the trauma needle and talked via radio with the hospital, my spiritual life-line came by vision to my mind. I could see my friend Troy Williams smiling on my couch with the missionaries, as they taught the gospel to my wife. Troy was a surgical nurse at Spartanburg Regional Hospital. I told the paramedics to take me to Regional, and to tell them to notify Troy Williams to be there at the ER. I knew that if I could only get a priesthood blessing, perhaps I could make it. The last thing I remember in the ambulance was a big beautiful soul of the black lady saying she was so sorry! I knew she couldn't help what had happened, it was just part of an unforeseen accident beyond anyone's control.

Upon arriving in the hospital, I was greeted by a female doctor and Troy. As she took my vitals she immediately asked what trauma surgeon I wanted? I didn't answer, but Troy asked her, "Is Dr. Cochran on call?" She said yes, and so he was dispatched. She took a pair of scissors and began to cut my clothes off. Her eyes grew a little wider when she realized that my white underwear was actually my temple garments. (For those who read this book and do not know, temple garments are special underwear that is a little longer than normal and have special meaning to the LDS temple worthy members. They serve as a protection from the world. They are worn with faith. They serve as a constant reminder to be modest, chaste, and unspotted from the world.) When she realized by the characteristics of the garments that they were religious in nature, she gave the scissors to Troy, of whom she also knew to be a member of the church, saying, "You can remove these special items for him." As she left the room to rush the surgeon's arrival, I told Troy, "I need a blessing." Troy looked at me fearfully and said, "I'll call your grandpa." I said, "No Troy," I need a blessing now!" By this time my wife had arrived. She was trying so very hard to be brave, but I could hear the fear in her voice. Troy seemed to immediately realize as well, that I needed divine intervention. I could tell that he was very apprehensive as to what he may be directed to say and to pray for me. He laid his hands upon my head and said the following: "Stephen Craig Mathis, in the name of Jesus Christ, and by the power of the Holy Priesthood, which I hold I lay my hands upon your head and bless you," His voice began to become confident, emotional, and full of power. He blessed me to live and to be healed. He commanded my body to recover. I was very happy to hear such words. I felt safe again.

Dr. Cochran is a very intelligent trauma surgeon. His blue eyes seemed to distill confidence to my soul. I could not have known then, but I find it ironic that this doctor who came to my aid then, would not have to lay the scalpel to me at that time, but would be called upon 20 years later to do an extraordinary surgery on me. More on that later.

Dr. Cochran told me that I had fractured my sternum and bruised my heart, and that I had a left ventricle hypertrophy. He said that he could feel the crack in my sternum, but that my chest muscles were so tight that there was no movement of the sternum fracture. He said that I would not need surgery for that, but my heart might be another issue. He turned me over to the Heart Center where a surgeon by the name of Dr. Dorchek, kept a solid vigil monitoring my heart. I think he felt like he might have to go in and fix something, at a moment's notice. I kept receiving Demerol shots to put me back to sleep. My butt felt like I had sat down on a hornet's nest with all the shots I was given. As the days went by, the words of that blessing rang true. I did not need surgery and I began to heal. I don't think I ever got the kink in my upper back worked out, because it still bothers me to this day. The pain and agony of a fractured sternum is one that I hope I never have to endure again. Every breath, and every moment, is excruciating. It took weeks to get better. Spartanburg Tech got a substitute instructor in place for me. I walked back into GE a couple months later, a different person. I knew now first-hand, how very short life can be. I began to look at things a lot differently. I reluctantly began teaching welding again and working third shift.

Angela had previously worked for Weldor's Supply House as a sales representative. I would go into the store to meet her and talk to her boss Roy Lipscolm on occasion. I began to look at those brand-new, red, shiny, Lincoln welders. I remember the Lincoln welding machine on the back of my dad's truck. I talked to Roy about one day getting a Ranger 10 LX diesel machine financed. I began to fantasize about maybe, just maybe... I would bring out of retirement that old Steve's Welding granite sign that I had been carrying around with me, from house to house.

I thought about getting a welding machine and trying to pick up some side jobs. I decided not to get it right then. Maybe I should just be content and wait a while. I was already working two jobs. I called Roy and told him I didn't think I was going to buy the machine. He said, "It's too late, I have already ordered it." I was shocked! I hadn't told him to order the machine. But, immediately I realized that I would now have to pay for it. That would mean picking up side jobs with my new welding machine. I would be a dishonest liar if I said anything other than I was excited about the inclination to do something with my own welding machine!

Quote from the Author

"Life is all about moments...and circumstances...when moments and circumstances present themselves, you must act with faith, passion, and commitment, to accomplish anything worthwhile."

So it began when my brand-new red welding machine came in. I financed a trailer to mount it on. I went back through some of the last possessions of my dad that we had managed to save in his wooden welding trunk. I found a striker, and a few torch tips, a Smith torch, a square, and his soapstone holder. There was also a scribe and a set of tip cleaners. These were cherished possessions from days long ago. I felt very fortunate to have them, for now they had a brand-new meaning and purpose.

All this happened about the same time period when I had gone into Geiss and Sons to look at the possibility of buying my wife a new diamond ring. I wanted to improve upon the little ring I gave her at the beginning of our lives together. Carlos Geiss is a shrewd businessman, and a master jeweler. He sold my dad a Rolex watch years ago, that my dad later had the initials SCM inscribed over his. It was his intention for me to receive it from him when I graduated from high school. Instead, I inherited it from my grandparents, after his death. As I looked at the different rings, I saw a half carat diamond, marquee cut stone, sitting on a beautiful ring, with princess cut baguettes on the sides. I told Carlos I wanted to lay it away. He obliged me and began to make mention of my dad and my grandpa. He said, after finding out that I too was a welder, that he needed some handrails made for, and installed at his Hilton Head Island jewelry store. He asked if I wanted to look at the drawings. I looked at them, and did a material take off. I priced the metal, the paint, and tried to envision the amount of labor it would take to do the job. I had the romantic idea that I could do that job in trade for the ring. He said he would buy the material, and I would do the labor. Looking back on it now, I should have charged him in excess of $15,000 in addition to the ring.

Things were moving so fast for me at that point. Two jobs and a moonlighting day job as my own boss! Angela and I were looking forward to meeting our fourth child. My brother Clint was interested in helping me, so I hired him part-time to help on those handrails. He had just gotten married to Lisa Gibson. He was having a hard time finding any work, anywhere. He was shy and a little backwards most of the time. Especially, since nearly being killed in a brand-new Pontiac Firebird, that mom had bought for him after daddy died. I would work the weekdays at GE and Spartanburg Tech, and we would fabricate handrails on my carport at home on the weekends. Carlos Geiss had sent me to Barton Iron and Metal to buy the tubing for the handrail project. It was there that I first met Darrell Robertson, the yard man, and Ben Swan, the son of the owner Garvin Swan. Barton Iron and Metal was a scrap metal yard that also sold new steel. I spoke to Ben and told him about our project. He seemed like a nice fellow. I began to think of the pros and cons of going into business for myself. I began to think of where I could get the business, and especially the repeat business. I knew I hadn't much money. But, I knew I could weld.

I thought of all that nasty equipment at the scrap yard. How everything, and every container, and every scrap trailer needed work. I thought about how abusive and hard the metal processing equipment was to itself. I remembered the garbage trucks, and the lumber yards that I had seen my dad work on, and at. I thought of concrete companies like Chapman Grading & Concrete.

I got me some business cards made and began to pass them out. Ben Swan was the first person to give me a job working on the junky steel, containers. I remember him coming up to me and my brother in that miserable pile of junk and mud saying, "Hey wait a minute! You are charging me $25 per hour, right? And, there are two of you, and only one welding machine! I can't pay $50 an hour to fix containers." He was very happy when I told him that I was including the extra labor, my brother Clint, all for $25 an hour. He began to get really excited and found us more, and more work.

I was burning the candle at both ends at this point. I was working the first, the second, the third shift, and cat napping in between them all. I was working in the junkyard when I got the call from my wife, and she was crying. She said that during the regular checkup the doctor could not find our baby's heartbeat. I didn't hear anything else. I just jumped in the truck and drove as fast as possible to the doctor's office. I walked in to find my sweet precious wife all emotionally undone, and spiritually torn apart. I asked the doctor and nurse to leave us alone. I knelt down, and touched her belly, that held our lifeless fourth child. I begged our Heavenly Father for His mercy and matchless power to restore our child. When the doctor came back in I asked him to check again. Our hearts broke as silence echoed across the microphone of the ultrasound machine. I remember the nurses telling Angela that they were worried about me. They said it was unusual to see a dad, or a partner, take this news so badly. And, badly, I did take it. I cried in my wife's arms. I took her home to prepare for the upcoming DNC the next morning. I went back to the junkyard to gather my tools and welding machine. I told Clint of our bad news, and he just looked at me, and said, "I'm sorry." I took a sledgehammer from up off the ground and tried my best to destroy the old junky container I was working on. I never had experienced so much rage. My arms exploded with each strike. But, after that explosive fit of anger, the fact still remained, that we had lost something very precious and dear to us. And, even though we never got to see our baby, in our hearts it was as if he/she already was part of our lives.

I called Carlos and asked him if I could get the ring early. I had just a little work to do on the handrail job. He said yes of course, and I gave that ring to my wife as she came into the recovery room after having the DNC. It was a symbol of our love and for what we had lost.

Time began to really move fast and yet so slow. I was trying to get over a bad car wreck, and loss of our baby. I never really could get used to working third shift. My body loved the daylight hours, and my heart missed my wife and kids at night.

Clint and Lisa asked me to sing, "I Swear," by John Michael Montgomery at their wedding. Lisa made a beautiful blonde-headed bride. Clint seemed happy but still didn't have a job. As I have gotten older now, my mind goes blank sometimes over every detail. But I do know this for sure, I began to hate the third shift, I began to really worry about Clint not having a job, and Clay my youngest brother constantly getting into trouble. There were great troubles ahead and great blessings ahead. I was in a state of being perplexed. Torn over what seemed safe and sure, and of what could possibly be, *IF* I went headlong into business for myself. I would take my breaks at night, and walk around GE. I would go outside to pray. I did not want to make a mistake. I worried so much about my brothers. I decided that I would ask for a leave of absence from GE, to get myself back into a healthier state of mind. I was told NO! I was told that I was a fool to even consider leaving GE. I went above my supervisor's head to inquire. The young engineer said he would check with his boss about a leave of absence. Once again, the answer was no. This time I immediately said, "Fine, then I quit!" The young engineer looked startled, and said, "You can't quit GE! Are you crazy?" I said, "I guess so! But I can quit, and I am quitting tonight!" They urged me to change my mind. They said if I ever wanted to come back, I could. That made me feel good, but I knew what I wanted. I wanted to reopen my dad's business, Steve's Welding Service! That was what I always wanted, and that's what I decided to do, right then and there!

My mom hit the roof, and then she came to my house asking if I needed mental counseling. She told me that my name wasn't "Steve," and that I was acting crazy. That I must be crazy to ever want to go back down those forbidden paths, back down the bad road of memories, to even think about owning my own business, much less to reopen Steve's Welding Service!

I let her throw her fit. I respected her opinion and knew that she was fearful for me. Everyone and everybody seemed to say, or flat out said, "Your daddy was the best. You won't ever be as good as he was." But I was resolute. My feet were already on the path that my heart had never let go of. The reality of leaving GE, and opening my own business full-time came crashing down quickly on me. I went from high-tech, pristine working conditions, to all of a sudden standing in the mud, working on junk. To be outside in a muddy, miserable junkyard, developing the art of putting twisted, rusty, and greasy containers back together, took a lot of common sense. I came up with jigs, and dogs, and ratchet binders to accomplish this task. You had to be able to access what to cut out, and what could be saved on the containers and trailers that were used to transport material. The large cranes used to load the scrap metal and junk were very abusive to the equipment.

I had guessed right. The scrap metal industry could keep a welder busy. I made fast friends with the Jewish boy named Ben Swan. He was one of three sons who ran the Barton Iron and Metal. I started off charging $25 per hour for mobile welding, which was cheaper than anyone else. The landfills and smelly containers were very challenging. Welding on rust is an art all of itself. I was evermore tempted to question, "Did I make the right choice?" But there was no looking back, because I was determined to make it work. We worked in the transfer stations, landfills, and at A1 Carting in the wintertime. We worked in the evenings and at night. There were times I had to stand guard with a shotgun killing the huge rats that came in a little too close for comfort while we were working on the garbage containers. I began to work Clint and Clay, as well as a host of others along the way. The work in the scrap metal fields proved to be constant, and repetitive like I had thought. I leased a small shop behind Dalton Carpet Warehouses. It was a small shop, but we were able to fab and paint things in there. I had a small office in the back and had begun to work for a variety of companies. I began to be able to afford tools, and things I could only imagine to be able to afford before. Shop welding machines, Portaband saws, chain falls, etc. As I worked then, it seemed like a lifetime of uphill, and baby steps. As I write this book, I see now, that it was at lightning speed. I was being led and prepared for one heck of a journey. And like Capt. Cole, in the movie, "Lonesome Dove," the vision that I was to behold at the end, would be one that I did not ever want to see. If I had known everything that would ultimately happen in the future, I just don't know if I could have, or would have, had the courage to embark on this journey.

Godfather Number Two

As time moved on, I began to look for a piece of land closer to the scrap yard to work on the containers and trucks. I spied a sign with **Dexter Cleveland** written on it on a wooded lot right next to the scrap yard. I had hired a young mountain man from West Virginia to be my welder's helper. His name was Craig Short. He loved to hunt, fish, and is a good friend of mine to this day. He moved back to West Virginia 10 or 12 years ago. Anyhow, when I showed him the property and the sign, he said, "Oh, I know Dexter! He is a good man. He owns half of Spartanburg, but he is good fellow."

Dexter Cleveland, a.k.a. Godfather, answered in his chipper voice, "Dexter Cleveland speaking." I introduced myself and explained that I wanted to use the wooden lot for a welding repair yard for the scrap containers. He said he would meet me in the afternoon the next day. Upon meeting Dexter, I found him to be an interesting character. He has a quick, wild sense of humor, but at the same time as sharp as a fox when it comes to business. He asked a lot of pointed questions, but he mixed it up with laughter and jokes. Swimming at the Y.M.C.A. and magic, are his past time passions, and he is quick to show a card trick or two. He agreed to the price I offered to rent the wooded lot. I presume because it was more money than he had in mind, or that he really didn't care as long as there was some activity generated on the land. I would pay $250 per month. My plan worked out as Barton Iron had no problem dropping off containers only a couple hundred yards away from its location. I got us out of the sun and the mud, and in the shade of those big oak trees. Dexter was driving a blue four-door Cadillac Seville at the time I met him. He is a small to medium build guy, balding a little, with obvious bowed legs. Although he walked a little bowlegged, he walked around with the authority of General Patton. I never could have imagined that at that moment, a lifelong friendship would develop as we shook hands.

Dexter and I hit it off immediately, and even though he was a very anal, complicated businessman, there seemed to be an underlying understanding that we had for each other. I couldn't put my finger on it, but something was there, hidden from the rest of the world, but very apparent to me, a friendship was being formed, and God was the author of it. His plan and purpose for my life was in full swing, and I didn't even realize the magnitude of it, yet. I am positive that God had prepared, in advance, my coming to know my Godfather; Dexter Cleveland.

And so, it began then, I would run a small welding shop, and work on the wooded lot for the scrap containers. It is hard to imagine the thrill of clearing and cutting a five acre lot while trying to figure out the good flat areas where we could work. Where would we put the driveway, etc? These were the days of my youth. As my business grew, so did I, physically. I was becoming a giant; very strong, very big, and very capable. I couldn't have known then that there was a reason for me getting so much bigger. It will be years before that reason would manifest itself. But for now, I felt like I was waxing strong in the Lord.

On the wooded lot, we had a big limb that grew on a 45° angle from an old red oak tree. We hung a chain-fall there. I didn't know how much it could hold, but I knew we unloaded 3500 pounds of steel from it in one lift. We worked like cavemen. Ben Swan would have us replace the steel tubing runners on the bottoms of his 30 and 40 yard roll-off containers. Also, Carolina Container Corporation and A1 Carting would have us do this job as well. The way we accomplished this, was by using a telephone pole and several old truck tires. If I didn't have enough people on hand, I would go down to the county jail and pick up released inmates off the street and pay them five dollars or so per hour to help flip those huge containers over upside down. We would pick up the telephone pole and stick one end of it underneath the nose or the hook area of the container. We would pick up on the pole and put a cut off short piece of the pole under it as a lever. Then we would painstakingly jump up or walk up the telephone pole until we had enough weight on the end of it to pick up the container. We would have a man there to place cribbing underneath. Then we would repeat the process, adding more cribbing underneath the side of the container until we had it high enough to be at its tipping point, and then we would use the truck, by tying a chain to the container and to the truck. We would soften the blow of the flipping container by placing the large truck tires along the sides where the container would land. It looked like something medieval, but it worked!

Joe Garrett and Jesse Black

I began to notice a big 'ole, burly, scruffy old man at church. His face and demeanor said to all who met him that he meant business. You could tell he had worked hard all his life. He had hands like a bear. He wore big black framed glasses. I had heard the name before, as a child. He had a lot of rental property and my dad had made mention of him, and his brother Beck. I spoke to him at church. He smiled and spoke back. I saw him off-and-on at church, but he wasn't active, or even a member. He smoked and cussed a little, and the missionaries had often taught him the gospel. His beautiful wife Lucille, and daughters Renita and Debbie, along with a son Eddie, were members of the church. Somehow our small talks began to get longer. The old man seemed genuinely interested in me and my business. I mentioned that I needed some clearing done at my wooded lot, and I needed to put in a driveway. He said he knew the right man for the job. Again, I had no way of knowing that he would be introducing me to another lifelong friend I had yet to meet; Jesse Black.

Joe Garrett and Jesse Black arrived at my lot complete with bulldozer and dump truck to put in my driveway. It was there that Joe saw that I was working as hard as a desperate fool could. He saw us using caveman/bull gang tactics to try and flip those big containers over. He mentioned that I should come over and look at an old fork-lift he had. It was a Ross 12,000 lb. lift truck. It was an antique lift, but a good one. When I saw it, Joe said he would take $5000 for it. He had an old five-ton, state flatbed truck as well. I wanted it for a junk yard truck. He said he wanted $1000 for it, and that he would finance them for me for the amount I wanted to pay each month.

I was overwhelmed by his generosity. I accepted and now I had the ability to lift the containers and unload the shipments of steel with ease. Things were going great.

We were doing an awesome amount of work. Then, the day came when Dexter Cleveland rolled up our driveway with a proposition.

Jesse Black

Lucille and Joe Garrett

The New Fabrication Shop

Dexter had already begun asking around the business community about me. I found this out from a couple of folks. He had inquired about how good of a welder I was, and asked if they thought I was worth putting any money behind. I did not know what the statement meant, but now it was coming to light.

He drove up that day and asked if I wanted him to build me a fab shop on the wooded land? He said he would let me design and build it. He explained, that if I did the construction, etc., my efforts would cut down on the cost. I was ecstatic and joyful, of course I would help! I was so excited. Everything was going so good. I was busy! My own business, S W S, was actually growing. I had no understanding of the fact, that although the waters were calm now, that the hurricanes were on the horizon. I met with Ben Swan at Barton Iron and Metal to tell him the news of my fab shop. He seemed happy for me and was excited that I would have a shop so close to him. I wanted to know that he was happy with my company and that I could count on work from him. He stated, as long as he had work, I would get it from him. That was enough for me. After all we were friends. I took him to places where I hunted, to film the birds, and eagle's nest that I had found on my hunts. Ben liked photography.

I met with Everett Matthews with Metal Builders Inc. We planned, and designed, a perfect fab shop. It would have loading docks and be designed for a five-ton bridge crane. In no time the building foundation was in, and the concrete poured. And at last, the day came when the prefab building hit the ground. We would work all day on the junk containers, and try to put the building up at night, and on weekends. My brothers Clint and Clay would be too tired or too busy to help at night, or on weekends. I would go and pick up the part-time jailhouse workers to help me erect the building. I hired a boy named Philip Cecil Schuyler to help me put it together. I remember taking pictures of myself along with the jailhouse crew in the snow, and bitter cold, piecing the building together, Clint and Clay would ride up to the job. They would get out of their sports cars and it would be obvious they had already been partying. They would say, "Hurry up! Big brother! What's taking so long? Hurry up and get it finished for us! We would help, but we are scared of heights!" And laughing they would get back in the car and drive right back off. I wondered to myself, how they could just reject the thought of helping me put up the building. Things were not going good with Clint or Clay at work. During the day Clint was becoming ever more resentful of my instructions. Clay would get mad and quit. Then he would come back. It was obvious that both of those boys didn't want me to be there daddy, or their boss.

They would make up every excuse to my mom, and living grandparents, as to why they could not help put up the building. They were scared of heights, tired; I was mean to them, etc. Finally, finally, I got it all put together. I was very proud. My mother, who had waited for 14-years to remarry, married a quiet man by the name of Tommy Alexander. Tommy was a master carpenter, and cabinetmaker. I was at my shop shortly after completing the framing, when mom and Tommy came to look at the shop. Tommy said that if I would get the two by four studs, he would help me frame up the walls of the office space. He came and helped me frame walls; well actually, I helped him. He was a very brilliant carpenter. The office took shape immediately. After that, I hired a sheetrock company to hang sheetrock, Tommy came back and hung the doors and installed molding. He also did the staining. I was so happy for his quiet, quality, professional help. He was a Godsend.

At last the finishing touches were put on the building. I used the same sign company that did my dad's signs originally. They remade the S W S eagle logo with the crossed spud wrenches on each side. The new sign was mounted proudly on the outside wall of the building facing the road.

Jesse Black brought his bulldozer and widened the drive, clearing more trees, and spreading the gravel for the huge parking and storage lot. I found two huge pieces of 30 inch I-beam from the junkyard. I cut and fashioned them to taper and reduce to a 10-inch base at the top. I painted them jet black. Jesse went with me to retrieve the cornerstone. We brought it from my house in the backyard, to its new home on 7056 White Ave. On those big black steel bases, we placed the old granite, Steve's Welding Service, sign up right again! Facing the world once again, full of promise

and hope. It sure was a proud moment for me! I remember the ease in which I retrieved the granite SWS marble sign that I had struggled so hard with as an 18-year-old kid, using a junky come along, and an old engine stand. The sign that had followed us everywhere we lived. A tombstone and a reminder of yesterday now sat in front of Steve's Welding Service's brand new welding facility on Asheville Highway. Standing back up again, it looked strong, invincible, and ready to take on the world. I was so happy. I was so emotional. I turned away at times to hide the tears. How I wished so badly that my dad could have lived to see this moment. Everything was looking up and looking fine. But Hell's fury was coming just around the bend. In the following days, I kept having the same dream. In my dream, I would meet my dad at the new shop. I would take the key ring off my belt, hand the keys to him, and say, "I got it all back, Daddy! I'm going to work for you now. Here it is, let's go!" I would only awaken to realize that dream was never going to be a reality. I felt all alone, but come what may, I knew God loved me, and I trusted in Him.

Late Night Construction

on the New Fab Shop

Bankruptcy, Trial by Fire

Time was moving so fast. I was working lots and lots of hours, doing more and more work for other people, and other companies. I could not ever get a sense of accomplishment, I never felt satisfied. It was like I was in a race, or in a hurry. I didn't know why. I just knew I was in a race against time. It was always like I had a deadline to meet. I could see my children growing up so fast. I wanted Casey Ann, my oldest daughter, to have her own room. I wanted my wife to be able to spend all her time with the kids. That wish came true with the news that God blessed us again with a fourth child. Angela was pregnant again! I cannot describe in beauty and detail, how I got such a rush of adrenaline every time my wife became pregnant! It was if my back got broader, my arms got stronger, and my heart made more room for the next beautiful soul to be sent to our home. I always knew that the souls that were sent to our home were care packages from heaven. I knew they were special, and I should have known they all would have special needs. They were being sent to the most kind, most remarkable, loving person I knew; my wife. Our baby Alex was born a remarkably beautiful, muscle-bound, baby girl. The doctor remarked, "This baby ain't nothing but muscle." If babies could come into the world in shape, fit and lean, she did! We had no idea then, that she would grow up to be an incredible athlete. A fast, fast, and enduring soccer player, track star, cross-country champion, and Scholar. That was all in the yet to see future.

I began to do work for Timmy Biggs with Biggs International Corporation. He is a textile machinery giant. He was very shrewd, and a cunning businessman. I began to weld on broken cast aluminum machine parts. These parts were being sent to France. We were also removing monorails out of Enoree Mills for Timmy. I had a crew of five or six men working for me. It was at that time, that a perfect storm was brewing for my demise. As a young, ignorant, welder, I couldn't calculate all the hidden costs associated with running my own company. I was a big walking bull's-eye for insurance agents, accountants, bankers etc. I got wrote into expensive workers compensation categories, not knowing that I could break out the non-skilled labor. My accountants were charging me $90 per hour, basically doing nothing to advise me on business and tax strategy. I was working too cheap. I wasn't contemplating the overhead charge that accompanies labor. My answer for everything was to work harder, longer, do more work, and get new work.

Things with Barton Iron and Metal had gone south, ever since I built my new fab shop. Ben told me that his dad said I was showing too much money! It looked like to the world that I was making too much money off of them! I was in shock. I told him that I came to him first with the news of my building. He seemed excited about it then, what was the problem now? About a week later Ben called me into his office and said, "We can't be friends anymore." I said, "Okay." He said, "No I'm serious! My dad says I should not be friends with the vendors and people who work for us!" I have to admit, in the words of this book, that it really hurt me. I really liked Ben. I felt like we were friends. I said, "You are taking yourself way too serious son." He said, "I cannot run a multi-million dollar business, and be friends with vendors." I just turned around and walked out. I didn't know it then, but money, power, and hurt feelings, turned me and Ben into bitter enemies. It is sad how fast human hearts can turn on each other. Shortly thereafter, Ben told me to come up to the scrap yard. He said, "I heard you are working for IMP now." IMP stood for Industrial Metal Processors. I had met a great guy by the name of Billy Scales, who worked for IMP. He had given me a little work to see if I could weld. He liked what he saw, so I was now repairing metal containers for him. So, I told Ben yes, I was working on some of IMP equipment. Ben said, "Oh, no you don't! You don't work for the competition!" I said, "Ben, you have cut back on the amount of work you give me. I have a shop to pay for and I have employees to look after. I gotta work for anybody who has something for me to do." Then Ben turned to me, and said something I will never forget, he said, "I put you in business, and I can take you out!" I told him, "We'll see about that!" And that's about as quickly as I lost our friendship. All the hard work we did for Barton Iron and Metal. All the containers that I repaired, all the scrap trailers, all the containers that I built new from scratch… Our friendship went away as fast as it took you to read these lines. After all these years, after all the changes in our business lives, things never got reconciled between us. Ben is now married with kids, he drives around in a Ferrari, and even though we both have been through so much, even though our youth is gone, we still don't speak. Maybe one day we will speak at the Fresh Market, or at a restaurant. Maybe one day, Ben won't jump up and run out of Panera Bread when I sit down at the table next to him. Maybe one day we can, and will, forgive each other. Maybe…

So just that quick I lost my main customer. And, just that quick that crooked, dirty rotten, Timmy Biggs decided he would not pay me the money he owed. I could not believe my ears with the news that Timmy had decided not to pay my bills turned in for work. Why? He had always paid. Why all of a sudden now, was he doing this? It turns out that Stanley O'Kelly, a purchasing agent for Timmy, had a nervous breakdown and was being treated for alcoholism. So, Timmy, although one of the richest men in the state, decided that even though he himself had signed the purchase orders for the work, that he would pay only $.50 on the dollar for all invoices. I talked to Bart Simpson, Timmy's mouthpiece. I asked him who would be able to settle for $.50 on the dollar. I went charging into Biggs International ready to fight. I said, "Guys, I need my money now. I owe taxes on the entire payroll paid out on this product." By that time, a little-bitty man with a scar down his face peeped in the door and whispered something to Coltrane, the vice president, and George Boswell, the corporate attorney. I didn't know it at the time, but that little-bitty man was the great Timmy Biggs, himself. He is very lucky that I did not know it was him. I would have given him a new perspective on how it feels to be cheated. I called my attorney's office, and they informed me to get in line to sue Timmy Biggs. Many, many, people had the same problem I was experiencing, and it would take one year to get into court. I didn't have a year. I had the IRS sending me letters demanding money for payroll taxes. Money was tight. We needed groceries, baby food, etc. It seemed like an impossible task each week to make payroll. Clint and Clay would work a while and get mad. Clay would leave and Clint would usually stay around but would be angry and unapproachable. He was gambling all of his money away at Mike's Café on the weekends and telling everyone that I wasn't paying him enough. That he wanted nice things, a house, etc. He lashed out at my other employees. Wouldn't listen to anything I said. He didn't know it at the time, but he was bringing more money home than me. A lot of weeks, I didn't get a check at all. One day I told Clint if he didn't like me or the people he was working with, to just go home, and that I didn't need him. He looked at me and said, "I thought this business was OURS?" I asked him how many bills he had paid. How many weekends did he work? Did he help build the business, or just simply get his check and go home? He left angry. I sat down feeling enormous grief and stress. How would he make it? How would I make it? How would SWS survive? How could I ever reach my brothers with daddy gone? How did everything get so hard and out of control?

I went to my accountants and told them that every time I called the IRS, I got put on hold, but that I had finally gotten in touch with an agent who said I could pay the $9,800.00 back at $900.00 per week. The accountant said that the payments were okay, but if I missed one week, they could come in, seize, and levy my property. I was scared to death! They suggested after looking at my finances, that I could possibly do a plan called Chapter 11. It was a form of bankruptcy, but it would give me five years to pay back everyone we owed, without getting my assets seized. It seemed like, maybe, it was the right thing to do. It was in fact, the craziest, most ridiculous thing to do, but I wouldn't know that until after I did it!

I walked into the bankruptcy attorney office of Mr. John Fort. The first thing he said to me was, "Steve Mathis, I remember him. I represented him in his bankruptcy. He killed himself, right?" His words were like a red-hot branding iron burning my heart. Yet, I sat there and let him talk. He said that for $5,000.00 he could get my Chapter 11 case underway and filed. That was exactly what Timmy Biggs' latest offer was, so I took the settlement from Timmy and gave the money to the attorney. I never knew what was to come. I had to list everyone and everything I owed. I had to put yard sale value on my clothes and home furnishings. I had to swear to the truthfulness of my financial affidavit. I faced a $500,000 fine if I was caught lying or hiding anything. It made a lot of people angry to be listed. Even the minutest amount of debt had to be identified, personal and business. A lot of people didn't understand. They thought I was doing well! I remember Dexter Cleveland came and sat by my side at the Federal Court building during the hearing. My lawyers told the judge, "Your Honor, Mr. Mathis has always continued to pay an honest tithing to his church, even though he has a lot of bad debt that he cannot collect. Most clients want to hide assets. He has always insisted that everyone gets paid." I didn't see how my attorneys, Sharon Butler, and Sid Wike, could be impressed with a man in bankruptcy, but with their statement, the judge said, "It is ordered!" And with the crack of his gavel, my Chapter 11 was underway. It felt as though I had been stripped off naked and publicly flogged. Everywhere I went, I felt like folks were talking and whispering.

I took comfort in this one thought: When I was a child my dad was in this same place. I could not, and would not let it beat me. Life is too important! I was very aware, at this point, that I would have to walk the same road my dad had walked. I did not understand why. I just knew I was there. I knew that without the grace, mercy, and goodness of God, I would be destroyed. I knew that I must be faithful. I must continue to call upon the Lord. I was in the heat of the battle for my family's survival. I could not become weak, and I couldn't let my guard down for an instant.

At this point, all of my employees were fighting, as once again, the return of Clint and Clay, kept the trouble making and intimidation going strong. The day came when I simply told everyone to go home and I would call them when I needed them. It seemed that every man that worked for me had a gun in his lunchbox or toolbox. It was truly pathetic how no one could get along.

Life's most important lesson:

After this, I was working on a huge I-beam that Robbie Chapman had given me from Chapman Grading & Concrete, it was rated for 5 tons, and it was long enough to span my entire shop floor. I just had to figure out how to hang it. I was welding on it when I saw the old man, Joe Garrett, walking up by the roll-up door. I could see in his hand, the letter from the bankruptcy court. I said to myself, "Oh, boy, this isn't going to be good!" As the old man walked in, I was under the weight of the world. He continued to walk right up to me, lean down, adjust his thick rimmed glasses, and said, "Boy, are you in trouble? What's wrong? How can I help you?" I replied, "I will pay you, Joe!" Then he said, laughing, "I'm not here for the money, boy! I'm here to help you." The old man walked around the shop, pulled himself up a chair, and just sat down there and went to sleep. Suddenly, I didn't feel so alone. For the first time in a while, I felt like I had really found a true friend.

Old Joe Garrett spent the rest of that day with me. In fact, we didn't spend a day apart for a long time after that day. He would come up to the shop and we would go get a pack of Neese's liver pudding, a loaf of bread, and eat lunch out in the shop. Other days, we would go to The Waffle House, and tell stories. It seemed as if me and Joe, or better yet, Joe and I, had been friends forever. Joe was always watching me, mostly when he thought I wasn't paying him any attention, like when I blessed the food each time before we ate, or when I went to the gas station and came out with something besides tea or coffee. He began to attend Priesthood classes with me at church. He began to listen to my testimony. He began to open-up to me about his personal matters. Joe had a huge hernia that happened when he flipped a bulldozer over onto him. He said, at that time, he could feel death coming upon him. He said he was able to shake it off of him, though. The hernia was huge and embarrassing to him, but I never really noticed it when we were running around. Joe had other issues. He needed a liver and was on a transplant list. He liked to smoke. It was a hard habit for him to try and break, over the years. Joe would always call me on days when he was too sick to come over to the shop. Somehow, my work kept coming, as I adapted constantly to all the changes I had been dealt. I had gotten an old safe in one of my deals with Timmy Biggs. I had a locksmith drill it out and get me the combination. It was there, in that old safe, that I created my own bank, "The bank of Steve." Back to Joe; after about 9 months to a year of mine and Joe's friendship, he began to accept the gospel. I told him that I would like to see him baptized as a member of The Church of Jesus Christ of Latter Day Saints. He began to take the missionary discussions, again. This time, after many years and many prayers, my friend Joe was submerged under the water and brought up as a new man. We stayed close to each other as we would bush hog pasture fields, talk, and dream of becoming cowboys, and cattlemen. Joe was an absolute godsend to me. Even though we were three decades apart in years, it seemed like we had been best buddies forever. Joe would often tell me to, "Sharpen my Pencil," and that I, "Couldn't Count," all in relation to me working too cheap. He would listen to the customers complain and cause trouble and he would say, "Don't get upset, son. Just smile and put that pencil to 'em, boy!"

Joe called me one day, after he had been sick for a while. He said, "I want you to come over here, boy. I want to talk to you." I had no idea what I was going to hear, but as it turned out, it was one of the most important lessons of my life. Upon my arrival, he said, "Son, all my life, I've worked hard. I spent most of my life worrying over where the next dollar would come from. The one thing I have learned is that sometimes the harder you try to make money, the harder it can become to make money." He continued, "All things, and everything, belong to our Heaven Father. He will bless you with what you need! So, from now on, I want you to walk down life's road like a little boy kicking a can along, without a care in the world, knowing that God will bless you according to his good measure and your needs." I caught hold of the thought of myself as the little boy kicking the can down the road, and I still try to live up to that vision today. I thanked Joe for his friendship, and that priceless advice. My sunny days with old Joe were coming to a fast end. I don't know if I couldn't see, or I wouldn't see it. I remember late one rainy night; I was driving on I-85, coming home from a 500-mile road trip from La Grange, Georgia. When my phone rang, I realized it was Joe. His voice was raspy. I could tell he was very weak. I asked him how he was doing, and he said the doctor said, not well. I told him to hurry and get better, and that we had things to do. Then he said something that tore my heart to shreds. I remember my tears falling like the pouring rain outside on my windshield. He said, "Boy, I want you to know that I have laid here all day on this couch praying for you. I see how hard you work, and I have asked our Heavenly Father to send down a blessing to you that there won't be room to receive it. I've asked God to open-up the windows of heaven, and pour it down upon you, son. So just keep paying your tithe, son, and let God bless you." I thanked him through my tears, trying not to let him know I was crying. I hung up the phone with the promise I would come and see him tomorrow. When the phone died, so did my restraint. All my soul and tears flooded. It broke my heart to know that my friend, Joe, was lying on his couch living his last hours, and praying for me! I went the next morning with a DVD player and the movie, "Dances with Wolves." I thought Joe would enjoy the movie. I wanted him to see the end where "Dances with Wolves" (Kevin Costner), is riding off from the tribe. One of his Indian friends is standing on the opposite mountain ridge, screaming to him, "Can't you see, you are my friend?" Two days later, the ambulance was called out to Joe's home. He died before they left the driveway. My wife came to the shop and told me he was gone. I just walked outside and looked at the sunset. I felt the space, now vacant in my heart, for my friend.

I stood with Joe, as long as I could. With his casket, that is. I followed the casket and the hearse to the church. He had a beautiful service. Joe was my friend, and I look forward to conversing with him again someday, when this life is over. He played a pivotal role in teaching me some of my most important life lessons. He taught me how to "kick the can on down the road by having faith in the Lord." I miss you, Joe!

Note to the reader:

Over the years, I have sat down to write this story of the Steel Meadow Farm, oftentimes, while on vacation with my family. There was no set time frame as to when, or if this book would ever be complete. Each time I began to write, I would go back and try to remember where I left off, or include details not mentioned before. This is the case with the next chapter. Although it may seem redundant, it was written at a different time, and includes pertinent details to this story.

SWS

June 29, 2012

I can remember my first glimpse of those three letters as a child that was painted on my dad's welding truck. They were stamped in his leather belt and painted on his hard hat. It was his company's logo, Steve's Welding Service. I would write them on all my school papers, sign my name and somewhere include SWS. To me, it was a symbol of pride, promise and the future. It was symbolic of my dad. I loved the logo, SWS, and it had always been my dream to reopen my dad's business. Actually, as a kid, it was my dream to become a part of his business; to be a connector, iron worker, and welder. I wanted to also help my father oversee the construction of big buildings. I longed for the day to be grown up enough to climb a column, to walk a naked steel beam, to make strong beautiful welds, and to run a crane. Those dreams never came to fruition because of his untimely death. I had witnessed the death of my father, the death of his business, the death of the dream of Steel Meadow Farm, and the mighty SWS dream. I witnessed everything being sold and my home torn down. The family farm and the big house were sold outright to thieves. We were a complete and a highly respected family, listed in Who's Who in the 1979 South Carolina edition. We were now in total disarray and spiritual chaos. After daddy's death, I had to start out at ground level in a common labor position, to become top helper, apprentice, to presently being a genuine certified multi-crafted welder, millwright, and precision millwright foreman. The Lord had blessed me tremendously. I could really work, and my welding skills had become very, very good. After I welded the big smoke stack for Sander's Brothers, at Hoechst Celanese, I went back to work for Fluor Daniel at Hoechst Fibers. I had been working out there for about a year when I heard that GE Gas Turbines was going to hire certified welders at their Greenville manufacturing plant. I applied, and out of 5,000 applicants, I was one of the 50 welders chosen. I loved working at GE, at first. It was also around this time that I got hired as a welding instructor at Spartanburg Technical College.

Stephen Terry Mathis   **Stephen Craig Mathis**

It was a very humbling and gratifying experience to be teaching welding at Tech. I felt like I was following in my dad's footsteps, and that was very satisfying to me. I thought, at that time as an instructor, of how I felt those years ago as a young man praying for inspiration and understanding to be able to weld. Now, to be teaching welding was an awestruck moment for me, to see how the Lord had blessed me. Following in my dad's footprints was just a taste of what was to come in my life. Those footsteps would be exact and bitter to tread. I just didn't have any way of knowing it at this moment in my life. I found myself working at GE and teaching welding at Spartanburg Tech. Also, at this time, my brother, Clint, was going to be married to Lisa Gibson. Clint had been involved in a very bad car wreck about 3-4 years prior. I believe as an answer to prayer, Clint did manage to get released from the hospital. No one knew what to expect as to his recovery. At the time Clint announced his intentions to marry Lisa, I had the misfortune of having a major car accident. After almost losing my life, I started to really pray about, and finally make a decision to go into business for myself, to finally reopen SWS. It was a glorious, fantastic experience to live my younger years, and to open my own business. Even though things started out really good, the Lord providing many miracles, and friends along the way to help me, because of bad debt in the economy, I still suddenly found myself being eaten alive in the jaws of the bankruptcy dragon. Those were some of the hardest, most difficult times of my life, but because of putting one foot in front of the other, refusing to quit, and gaining strength from the Lord, I managed to pay off my five year Chapter 11 plan in three years. However, my credit would remain ruined for the next decade. At that time, I could not see the future, but the Lord could. Even though the element of bad debt owed to me in association with failing textile plants had put me in bankruptcy, the Lord had led me to this situation, and through this textile demise, my businesses would become blessed.

Textile Town, Textile Ruin

Dictation: January 8, 2017 2:07 PM

At the dawn of America's textile/industrial revolution, industrialists and businessmen were looking for cheap energy and cheap labor. The south provided both. With the invention of the water wheel and jack shaft came the ability to produce horsepower and motion for free, as long as you had flowing water. The fast, steady, flow of the South Carolina, North Carolina, and other southern state rivers, proved to be excellent. Also, the abundance of farmers and their children provided a cheap supply of labor. These were hard folks, religious folks, prideful, with the dream of finding and living *The American Dream*. Spartanburg and the small rural communities surrounding it, flourished because of its ample rivers and large work force. Early entrepreneurs like DE Converse, began to build huge textile mills. The red southern clay provided an excellent source for sun dried bricks. Oftentimes, bricks were made on the site of these mills. The great rich wealth of "Southern Heart Pine," that grew up to a hundred miles inland from the coast provided excellent and outstanding sources of lumber for these huge mills. Initially machinery came from Europe, but it wasn't long until America started to produce textile machines on its own. The result began the miracle of the textile revolution and the industry of the south.

Jesse Black at Lockhart Mills

Cotton Mills became a way of life, a symbol of pride, and hard work for lots of folks. All my family seems to have gotten the experience of the hard work and sweat of the cotton mill. As the southern cotton blossoms were picked by hand and delivered in most cases by mule to the mill, the USA garment manufacturing machines ran 7 days a week and 24 hours a day. These cotton mill industries would build stick frame, A-frame houses all around the mill property to rent or finance them to its employees. Thus, the term "mill hill" came to indicate that you were born and raised, and lived next to the cotton mill. Places like Converse, Clifton, Cowpens, Pacolet, Pacolet Mills, Startex, Una, Beaumont, Lockhart, Monarch, Cliffside, Spartan, and Glendale only to name a few of these cotton mill rural areas that were derived and came to be.

My family worked as weavers, spinners, doffers, loom fixers, etc. The work was hot, sweaty, and loud, as hundreds of shuttle looms ran in unison. When I was born, the textile industry was in its prime, strong, vibrant, and alive. The term made in the USA was the world standard in the garment industry. The south was rich.

Spartan Mill

Spartan Mill, today.

The Self's, Montgomery's, Milliken's, Converse's, were amassing fortunes and becoming some of the wealthiest landowners in America, especially in the south.

An industry that had begun in the 1800's, and become so strong, would be brought to its knees in two to three decades of my life.

No one could see it coming. No one could anticipate the deals and the underhanded undertaking of the US government. Foreign lobbyist, uncensored payoffs, and campaign contributions to congressmen, began to open the doors to the wolves of the American business interest. American textiles would be sold out; imports from China, Pakistan, and India would flood the American market. Like a cancer, the textile industry was becoming sick, weak, and terminal. I was working at Hoechst Fibers as it came across the news that President Jimmy Carter had signed the NAFTA trade agreement. For the first time I realized we were in trouble. In the months following, announcements were made that some of the plants would be closing and moving to Mexico. To make a long story short, Roger Milliken's attempts to save the textile industry never came to fruition. Public campaigns to promote **Made in the USA** always seemed to come up short to the cheap price of products made in China. During the Bill Clinton administration the textile towns all went bust. I found myself in a struggling welding business in Chapter 11 Bankruptcy.

Leo Lopshire, fellow church member and friend, worked for me and tried to help me find new business. I had bought an aluminum smelter from Ozark, Alabama to melt scrap aluminum parts like engine heads, transmissions, etc. I decided to start another business. I called it Specialized Scrap Metal. I was cleaning electric motors for copper and other specialty reclaim of aluminum parts. It was hard and hot labor melting down the heavy oily scrap aluminum. We were doing everything we could to stay in business including working on trash cans, and making scrap deals on things to melt down. I welded the SWS logo in the metal ingot containers, and we began to melt and produce the SWS aluminum ingots. Leo contacted Jim Rivers with Milliken and Company and begged him to give my companies, the newly formed Steel Dynamics USA Incorporated, and Specialized Scrap Metal, LLC an opportunity to bid on their scrap metal and textile plant tear out jobs. And, as God would have it, Jim Rivers said yes! About the same time the textile plants were closing, a man named Dean Bemel with Limco Generator Industries, stepped in.

Many of the mills are being refurbished into apartment buildings.

Find more information about the ruin of Textiles Mills in a book found on Amazon:

Textile Town

https://www.amazon.com/s?k=textile+town&i=stripbooks&ref=nb_sb_noss_1

Betsy Wakefield Teter, Author

The Gaffney and Spartan Mill can be seen in ***Textile Town***.

Dean Bemel with Limco

Dean came to me at a time that I was desperate to replace my business that I lost with Barton Iron and Metal. Dean had some government contracts to build self-contained generator units for the Army Corps of Engineers. It was, or seemed to be, a great opportunity. I designed and fabricated some beautiful 40 ft. self-contained, sound attenuated generator units for the Army Corps of Engineers. I began to store new generators for Dean. Dean suggested that I could build him a generator warehouse and to do the warehousing and technical generator assembly and testing. It sounded great! I talked Dexter into building another 4000 square foot warehouse and loading dock for the generators. All went good right up until Dean got his own warehouse, and then he broke his one and only rule. I was to do the welding and fabrication and no one else was to do that on my property. Dean eventually had every other welder he could get doing the business, but me. He constantly made every effort to underbid my work. I was very proud of the work that we did, fabricating the generator units for government hydro-electric sites, and Army bases such as Chief Joseph Dam, as well as others. But Dean decided to backstab me, and tough times were, definitely upon me now. The smelter fire ran at 3 am in the morning to try and beat the summer heat. I often thought of how I would love to put Dean into that furnace. I felt like he truly deserved it. I had a little buddy working for me named Bobby Bright. Bobby was a strong, hardworking, little guy who worked right beside me. I loved my little buddy. He really got into the big fire of the hot smelter. He caught on to running it, and he worked it really well. Bobby and I became really close, as we worked those long hot hours together maybe a little too close. I loved Bobby like a son. I had at this same time the notion of starting my own scrap metal business. I thought, after all, I had made and fabricated a lot of pans and containers for the Swans; why not for me? I began working on the notion and counting the cost.

I talked to a friend of mine named Larry Wigington about going into the scrap metal business. Larry and I had been fierce competitors bidding on junk from Biggs International as the local cotton mills were closing down. Bigg's salesmen would tell me Larry's bid on junk, and then tell Larry my bid, so we kept walking each other up on the price. I finally came up with the idea to go to the big, rough, looking guy, Larry, and negotiate a deal with him. I had an idea that we could work together! I would bid low and not go up. Biggs would sell the machinery to Larry and he would sell the irony aluminum to me! My plan worked really well, and it was honest payback to Timmy Biggs. Anyhow, Larry said "Steve, you are going into the scrap metal business at the worst possible time ever! Prices are terrible, junk is bringing now what it was in the 1950's. Fuel is high." But my daddy always told me, "Son, you gotta walk sometimes when everyone else is running, and you gotta run sometimes when everyone else is walking." I thought that made excellent sense. Barton Iron had begun to charge container rental and everyone hated them for it. I felt strongly that I could get business, but how to go into the scrap metal business broke and busted was another issue. I didn't have to find out why; I just had to find out how.

A Few Certifications.

George Gillespie

I met George Gillespie when I started my welding business. He ran a trash disposal service by the name of A1 Carting. His wife, Kristi, and I attended school together and she was also friends with my wife. George would let me work on his trash trucks and containers.

George is a redheaded, northern Irish, and a hot blooded businessman who has a passion for both hard work, and his family. I had the idea to ask him to start a scrap metal company with me. He said he thought it might be a good idea. So, he had his father check his connections for some scrap metal Lugger trucks. Before I knew it, he had found one up north and had found another extra body that he said he would put on one of his garbage trucks as a spare. We rode around some, looking for used Lugger cans or containers for the scrap metal. George had his lawyer drawing up papers for the partnership. That's when things started getting difficult. There was really no way for me to keep up with the capital investment George wanted to make on the onset. Also, we had differences in our marketing strategies that posed problems. George was hot tempered and so was I. Our wives were concerned we would lose our friendship. At last, George decided to stick with the waste hauling business and agreed to finance me the two Mack trucks so now I was in bigger debt. But nevertheless, I had scrap metal trucks bought for me and that was a huge piece of the puzzle solved. I am thankful for the help George afforded to me at that time. We are still great friends to this day. "Thank you, George, for your friendship, and for all the help you gave me."

Meanwhile, Bobby won a gun on a tip board at Pudge's Bar and Grill over in the UNA area of Spartanburg where he was staying. He walked to the bar and picked up the new and unloaded gun that he had won. As he walked home in the dark, three men from the bar followed him. They jumped him several blocks away, beat, him, robbed him of the gun, and his money. They kicked and beat my dear friend in the head with a 4x4 piece of wood. They pulled his pants down so that he could not run, and they beat Bobby until they thought he had stopped breathing. I got the call late that night from his mom. Bobby is now a severally brain damaged man with a feeding tube in his stomach. He is bedridden and has been for years. I visited him for a while, long enough to realize Bobby would never know or remember me again. I miss my dear friend so much. I was devastated that had happened to him and that I wasn't there. My heart and mind relived the beating that he must have taken over, and over. I know I should go see Bobby now, but I just can't. I hope to find the courage, someday. Grieving over Bobby and working off a Chapter 11 Bankruptcy, paying for a generator warehouse that I didn't need, and now financing scrap metal trucks, was to say the least, nerve racking and scary.

Kristi and George Gillespie

Kerkle Enterprises

I'm pretty sure it was George Gillespie who told me a scrap metal company in Atlanta, Georgia had some Lugger pans for sell at Kerkle Enterprises on Fulton Street. I called and talked to old man Kerkle. He sounded pretty nice and said he was going straight over to roll off containers and would be getting rid of all of his Lugger containers. He told me to stop by and see them, and so I agreed.

SCDOT

As I said before, I was paying Leo Lopshire to try and contact potential clients on the internet. He somehow stumbled across the fact that the SCDOT was going to take bids on their scrap metal accounts. I told Leo what I felt we could pay per ton for steel and what I could pay per pound for the aluminum road signs. I didn't think I had a chance at actually getting those accounts, but because I had bid aggressively and wasn't charging container rental or trucking fees, all of a sudden, I was winning all of the bids across all of the counties across the state. They asked me how long it would take to service the accounts and deliver containers both for steel and aluminum. I said about three months, with no idea whatsoever of how I would pull it off. I didn't have any containers and life was starting to go 100 mph. The stress and nervousness of how I would pull it off really started to pull on me day and night. I knew my Heavenly Father was leading me. I knew things were happening to me in miraculous ways. But I have to confess, it was very, very, nerve-racking.

CDL License

I suddenly realized that if I was going to be in the scrap metal business, I had to be able to drive a big truck. If I was going to do work for Milliken and Company, I had to be able to move my own equipment. It made me physically sick to my stomach to think of trying to drive a big CDL semi-truck. The thought of having to test and having to learn to drive was something I procrastinated doing. I didn't have time to sit down, much less study. But I knew that I must do it. So, I reached out to my friends and began to talk to them about it. Larry Wigington said I could borrow his truck to take the driving test. I was very happy to hear this because I didn't have a tractor or a trailer. I had so much going on, trying to come up with pans or containers, trying to bid work for Milliken, running my welding shop, and melting scrap. I was working 14 to 16 hours every day. My family was growing-up; my wife had become pregnant with our fourth child, Alexandra. I was scared to death. During this time, I began to read a book called, *The 48 Laws of Power*. It was a book that would give me some strategic ideas to overcome my problems. One of which was to use subcontractors!

Wigington Scrap Metal

After Larry Wigington said I could borrow his truck, I started to study the CDL guidelines manual. I went to take the test. I was really nervous. The pre-trip test part went pretty well. I thought I was doing a good job when the test instructor looked at me, and she said "Mr. Mathis, you have already told me more than enough. You have told me more about a big truck than anyone ever has. Let's move on to the road test, shall we?" I took the road test and couldn't believe that I actually passed! Truck driving came very natural to me, the Lord opened the eyes to my understanding, and it was as if I had been driving a truck for years.

At the time all of this was going on, I got a call from Mr. Jim Rivers from Milliken. He was offering me a chance to look at a big, stainless steel machinery tear out job at Magnolia Finishing plant. I really was worried about how I could possibly man such a job. One of the 48 laws of power is: Let others do the work and you take the credit."

Larry Wigington

Suddenly, the light bulb went off and I had an idea! A really good and big idea. I would partner up with Larry Wigington. Larry had a large crew and experienced men. We had always competed against each other for jobs and I was impressed by his operation. He had men, hard workers who treated him like their general. Larry was a great big man, and the Army had given him both the experience and the vision of how to get and give respect.

I approached Larry about the possibility of us working together.

Larry was very interested, and then something unbelievable happened. Something I will never forget. This is the day our friendship was forged. He said, "Son, look me in the eyes! I won't ever cheat you! If you can handle the neckties, I can handle the work! You handle the red tape, you deal with the plant engineers, you submit the bids, and I can handle the work."

So that day, we came to an agreement, and we went to Milliken to look at the job. Larry told me he could tear out the equipment for free and he would keep the money for the stainless steel. I would use my pipe welding and millwright experience to help with support with de-energizing the equipment, process piping, etc. I figured in what I thought it would take to do the job, if and when Larry backed out. So, I bid $60,000.

Jim Rivers called and asked me, "Are you sure? It is about half of what the next lowest bid given." I told him that we were honest and hardworking and could do it for what I asked. With that he said we were awarded the job, and the flood gates would soon open wide for all of the Milliken Plants operating in South Carolina, and Georgia.

Soon after getting word that we were awarded the job, I again, got a call from Jim Rivers that Ken Daniel wanted to meet with me at Magnolia. Ken was a high-level supervisor and he said that the environmental people were concerned about the tear out, because of possible ground contamination at the plant, as we moved out the equipment. This was a big problem because it would drastically slow down the job, waiting to load out each piece onto a trailer or container, immediately after its removal. I was very upset and told Ken that I would get back with him. As I left the plant, I did what I would usually do when faced with big problems. I went driving and prayed to my Heavenly Father. I listened to beautiful music like Jim Brickman, Kenny G, or my favorite, Miles Davis. I discovered as I listened to Miles Davis, I could focus on paperwork, bids, planning, etc. As I prayed and listened, I saw a picture in my mind of the large 9x40 ft. by 3/16ths inch sheets of carbon steel that I bought from Birmingham, Alabama to build scrap metal containers and such, for the scrap metal companies. In my mind, I saw a big floor pan, much like a giant oil pan, so I got the inspiration from God and I went to work planning. I told Ken that we would weld, and build on site, a 40 x 40 feet floor pan out in the parking lot, outside the building. It would be welded solid and be completely leak proof, it would be surrounded and curbed by 4 x 4 inch angle iron. It would handle and catch any fluid from the machinery. Ken and the environmental staff loved the idea! And so, I picked up more work from Milliken! Things were beginning to be very promising. The first job went very well. I was being asked to look at more, and more, work for Milliken. I was keeping Larry busy. I was keeping my welders busy. Clay and Clint were constantly fussing and fighting on the job. Clay occasionally came to work in no shape to work. I was hoping they would straighten up this time, without having to be fired again. Ken Daniel told me he wanted me to look at bidding a big stainless steel welding and fabrication job. It was an impressive series of stainless steel platforms and ladders for a new print line that Milliken was putting in at Magnolia. The job I bid was to be time and material with a 20% markup for all material purchased. This was significant because stainless steel was very expensive. As I bought the material, the 20% was adding up to be a good profit. Jim Rivers had set my company up as payable immediately, so I was able to keep up with the job. The job ended up being over $300,000. I couldn't find good help for all of the fabrication work. Larry was doing good work on the entire tear out. Whatever he would bid, or say what he needed to do a job, I would simply double the price and we were all doing pretty well. Clay and Clint continued to fight, argue, or goof off when I wasn't on site.

The supervisor at Milliken that I was working with directly told me that I was at a crossroad. He could see my dilemma. I had to stay the size I was, or I would have to make a decision to get some more help to supervise and watch after my men when I wasn't on site. It was a constant ongoing struggle. I was good at getting and doing work, but I was being victimized by my employees whenever I had to leave. It was a struggle that my daddy always seemed to have to go through, as well. I went down to Atlanta to look at the Lugger pans at Kerkle Enterprises old man Kerkle acted as if he was my long lost friend or grandpa. He said he would sell me all of the Lugger pans I wanted for $500 for the 10 yards, and $700 a piece for the 20 yards. I had found the containers for the DOT bid! But how would I get them from Atlanta to Spartanburg? I talked to Larry Wigington about it and he said he would let me borrow his truck and 50 foot low boy trailer. The day I went to Atlanta to buy some of the containers, we stacked them high. It was so nerve-racking pulling all of those containers through downtown Atlanta on Saturday. Traffic was horrible, but by the grace of God I got my first load home. Shortly after I had bought my first load, I got a call from old man Kerkle. He said he really, really, wanted to help me out. He said to bring him what cash I could and he would finance all the containers I wanted. He said he had some old trucks and equipment that I could look at, too. As I went each week to Atlanta, I financed two old Mack trucks with Lugger beds, and an old excavator with a scrap claw attached.

I began to paint and place the containers at the various DOT locations. I was also fabricating and building containers, as well. I still had Clint and Clay working for me and a good worker by the name of Mike Sellers (Pony), who worked for me awhile and became a good fabricator and welder. Pony built a lot of containers for me; however, he did not like the junk and equipment, and the scrap metal jobs. Pony ended up moving to Oklahoma, as he fell in love with an Indian gal he met on the internet. I will always remember Pony as a dedicated worker, and a good friend. Anyway, back to Barry Kerkle.

As soon as I had bought all the containers, I was going to have to have the equipment moved home. Oh, and by the way, I had another friend by the name of Wayne Durham, a logger by trade, who agreed to move the scrap equipment to Spartanburg for me on his lowboy trailer.

About a month or two later, old man Kerkle called me and said he had bought some equipment and he needed all of his money immediately! I told him that we had a deal, and I would pay him monthly payments as we agreed. He became very angry and demanded it all. He had once sat in his office and bragged about busting ears, and cracking heads with his baseball bat, at his Fulton street junkyard when people gave him trouble. Now, I was getting to see the ugly side of Mr. Kerkle. I told him again that we had a deal. He sent threatening letters and he even sent two goons dressed in leather jackets and sunglasses, driving a Lincoln Continental, to my shop one day. I suppose they either were dressed up like members of the mob, or they actually thought they were members of the Kerkle mafia. I didn't like the looks of these two as I saw them drive up in the parking lot late that evening. So, I met them at the office door with my pistol grip 12-gauge pump shotgun. They said they were there to collect Kerkle's money! I said, "Y'all boys are out of luck!" I said, "I got to deal with Barry and he knew all along what it was." They looked at each other and they said they would be back. I told them not to be back. They dropped a 44 hollow point bullet on the steps as they left. I continued to pay Barry Kerkle in full, month by the month, just like our agreement stated.

Farm Lake

I had always dreamed of making my wife and kids happy. I always dreamed of having a house big enough for each one to have a bedroom all their own; especially Casey, my oldest daughter. She had always shared a room with her siblings. With the Milliken work, and the Milliken fabrication work, I was starting to make good money. I had managed to pay off the Chapter 11 debt early and started to get back on solid ground. Angela and I were looking at houses and daydreaming when we drove into the Farm Lake community. We saw a beautiful two-story brick house for sale. It was so beautiful and wonderful. It had a fence in the backyard making it perfect for the little ones. We talked to the realtor and made an offer, which was accepted. However, when we applied for credit, my credit was no good because of the Chapter 11. So, I went to a secondary lending company, and they said no. So, I had an idea, I told the secondary lending company that I'm going to pay $50,000 down. And guess what? Yep, they said yes. So, we moved into the house and started to go to the newly formed Boiling Springs Ward. Times were very hard, very good, and very stressful. But we were living the dream we wanted for our kids, and our love was increasing. Angela, after two years, became pregnant with our fifth child! I remember how she grabbed my hand, looking at the ultrasound, "It's a boy!" She yelled. We both cried over the fact that we were going to have a boy. Our plate and cup were running over.

Stephen Cross Mathis

Our first baby boy was born on a cold February day. It was a difficult birth for him and my wife. Angela's blood pressure began to drop and the nurses were concerned for her. A few minutes later the doctor arrived and said the umbilical cord was wrapped around our son's neck. She suggested we pray. I will never forget that moment of terrible fear as both mother and baby struggled together to make a miracle happen. The doctor, nurses, me, and Angela, held hands and prayed. So much love, emotion, and determination, gave way to celebration, as my son Stephen Cross Mathis began to cry, after making a hard fought entry into the world. After a few hours, the nurses told my wife that they were going to take him to get his hearing checked. Angela started crying and saying, "He can't hear!" I said, "Yes he can! Don't worry!" The nurses brought him back a perfectly healthy little boy.

It was snowing and cold the day we brought him home. He first had to visit the SWS offices while his mother did the payroll. She was an incredibly strong and determined mother. So, my son technically went to work on his first day into the world. And so it was, we took our little boy home, whom I knew absolutely nothing about or what to do with. I felt the weight of responsibility now for raising a son. I wasn't afraid of much in the world, I had already gone through some very tough times, but now it seemed I was absolutely terrified of this little boy! I had to be a good, successful father, not just to him but to my girls as well. I just had to.

We named him Stephen Cross Mathis after his great-grandmother, Elizabeth Cross. I knew that a name was a heavy cross to bear, as I had taken on my first name as Steve. It was a constant reminder of my dad. I wanted Cross to always remember that his name was everything, and that the cross Jesus Christ bore for us was a noble cause to follow. These were the golden years, and the hardest years of my young life. I spent, and had unlimited strength, and energy. I was waxing strong in the Lord and becoming large in stature. I knew that I was being blessed by the Lord both physically and mentally as well. I would ride Cross in my Mack truck when he was a little baby. He would ride in the car seat right up in the front. When he began talking, I taught him to say, "We haul junk, but we don't take any junk." It was hilarious. We would pull the big truck over at a playground along the way, and out of that big ole Mack came this pint size little dude with blue jeans, work boots, and ball cap, ready to play. Those were some of the best days of my life. Looking back, reflecting on it all, I find it ironic that my dad died on a cold February day, a day that it started to snow so very gently. It was also a cold February day, snowing very gently, when I brought my little boy home from the same hospital where my dad died. It is so true, what Job said, "*...the Lord gave, and the Lord hath taken away; blessed be the Name of the Lord.*" (Job 1:21)

Juan

January 8, 2016 6:18 a.m.

One bright sunny day, there came this long haired, skinny, Mexican boy named Juan, and his brother Uriel. They were young looking little chaps on bicycles. As they came up to me in the shop, they were trying to look all hard and tough. But I could tell they both were nervous, as they kept shifting their eyes at each other. "We cutting steel!" said Juan, I asked, "You are?" He said, "Yes/Si, we cutting steel for you." I don't know how they knew I was cutting scrap metal to size for the steel mill, I guess they were hiding watching me to see what kind of work I was doing. I knew these boys were full of it, in other words, lying about knowing how to cut steel. So, I said "Okay, go ahead, go out there," and I pointed to the steel pile. I watched for about an hour as these two desperately tried to "light" the torches. It was hilarious and pitiful at the same time! My heart went out to these two little amigos. They were willing to try anything to get a job. I went out there after a while and said, "You cutting steel?" They both dropped their shoulders and they looked at their feet. I took the 6 ft. torch away from Juan and he started to walk away. I said, "Oh no, amigo, get over here!" I lit the torch and started cutting the steel the two watched intently. After a moment or two, I handed it back to Juan. He wasn't exactly cutting steel, but I would say he was melting it. I walked off and let them have the rest of the afternoon to try to figure it out. At the end of the day, they had a small pile of steel cut. Juan asked, "I cutting steel tomorrow?" and I said "Yes." They were overjoyed, jumped on their bikes, and pedaled down White Avenue. Today had been a success for them. They told a lie, been caught in the lie, and still left with jobs they did not know how to do. I did not know it at that moment, but I had just met a friend for life. Juan came every day and worked as hard as he could to learn the scrap metal business. It was very hard for us to communicate, because he spoke little English, and I spoke even less Spanish. He got better and better at cutting steel. One day, he and Uriel had a big pile going. It had gotten so tall they couldn't see each other because of its height. Uriel threw a piece he had cut over the top of the pile by accident.

The piece of 2 inch angle iron, hit Juan upside his head so hard that it busted his eardrum, and knocked out his front tooth. The little fellow was in obvious pain, I told my secretary to take him to the doctor. Later that afternoon, I saw him back out at the steel pile cutting steel. I was so impressed by his ability and desire to work. Not just to work, but to give everything he had to make me happy with him.

One day they ran out of work, and when I got back to the shop they, the two brothers, had cut some evergreen branches, tied them together to make a broom, and each one was sweeping the shop. I had never witnessed such a desire to stay busy as these two lads.

Another time, I bought some metal from Watkins Brothers Fab Shop. It was a big pile of iron I had agreed to cut up on site. I left Juan and Uriel that day with their lunch. Later that evening, I got tied up on a Milliken tear out, and with traffic. I was going to be late getting back into town. I called my friend Joey Macelraft, who I had worked with in my early years at Hoechst. I said, "Joey can you go pick up, or check on Juan and Uriel?" It had started snowing heavily, and had already gotten dark. I was worried they would be upset thinking that I had forgotten them or just didn't care. I was fond of them, especially Juan. I treated him like he was my son.

Joey called and said "You ain't gonna believe this!" My heart dropped. I asked, "What is it?" He said, "Them crazy Mexicans have gathered up firewood, built a big ole fire, and they are still cutting steel!"

And, so it would be for the next few years to come, they worked so very hard for me, and the company. Uriel finally got homesick and moved back to Savannah, Georgia. Juan stayed. One day I caught Juan sitting up in the new excavator; the one Larry Wigington had found for me. It was a nice scrap machine. A Deawoo,

220 LC3, with an orange peel grapple, and a five-foot magnet package. Larry found it in Belton, South Carolina. A bank had foreclosed on it. Larry talked Charles Mills, another scrap metal dealer who had just recently sold his scrap company to CRG, into financing the machine for me for $50,000. It was a steal, another gift from my Heavenly Father. Anyway, Juan looked shocked when I caught him eating his lunch up in the crane. He was embarrassed, and didn't know whether to jump out, or sit there like a cat caught in a fish bowl. I said, "Turn on the key amigo." He said, "No," and I said "Yes/Si, amigo." I taught him that day how to run the scrap crane. He was the happiest, most powerful, little Mexican, this side of Christendom. He was becoming and will always be, the best worker I ever had, but more on that later.

Uriel

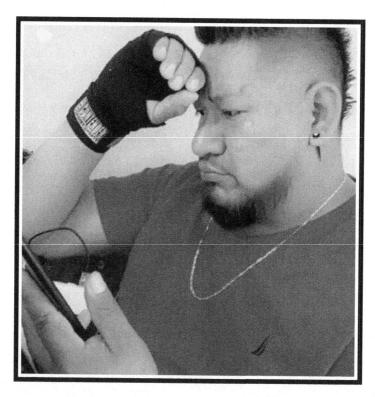

Homecoming

And so, it was, as my scrap metal business grew, my emphasis shifted from a lot of welding and fabricating, to a lot of textile plant junking and scrap metal reclaim. The junk was pouring in. Dexter Cleveland financed me a brand-new Bobcat and Labounty scrap metal sheer. We could go right into the mills with that machine and munch, crunch, and tear out equipment fast. My business was on fire and out of control. I didn't know what was around the corner, but it began with a casual remark, just a simple statement that happened to come out of my secretary's mouth. She said, one day around lunch time in my office, "My mother-in-law toured your old house, the one you grew up in." I said, "Really?" She said, "Yes, it's for sale!" I said, "No it is not. Steve Abbott told me months ago that a doctor bought it." She said, "No it's for sale!" She made a call, and said, "Remax has it listed." My heart about exploded. Tears, memories, and heartache raced through my mind, flooded my eyes, and filled my soul. A promise made twenty years ago, by a small, penniless, eighteen-year-old boy to his two little brothers, came back into my mind like a hot brand burns into the side of a helpless animal. That promise, "We will get it back, one day, by God I swear, I'll get it back!" I had given up over time on the reality of that promise. It felt like the Tyrants would never sell it, but right here, right now, in this moment, I had the chance!

I called Rich Tyrant and he didn't answer. Then, I called his dad, Billy. I said "Billy," don't let Rich sell that house to nobody! I want to take a look. I'll pay full price!" He said, "Okay I'll tell him." My heart was pounding so hard. I waited in suspense for the call back to set up the appointment. A thousand thoughts were going through my mind. How would I pull this off? Was it of God, or was it just another tool of the Devil to torment me? We were in a lot of debt. We lived in a nice place. We liked the Boiling Springs Ward and the schools. I called my wife and said, "Angela, you ain't gonna believe this, but the old house and the land is for sale! The Tyrants are selling." She said, "You're kidding." I told her I wanted her to go with me to look at it, and she said okay in a very nervous voice. Rich called me back later that afternoon and said the house was about to go under contract, but he hadn't signed anything, "yet." I told him not to, until I got an opportunity to look. He agreed to let me look the following morning. He explained to the potential buyers that I just grew up there, and I just wanted to look again. I don't think I slept hardly any that night waiting to go back home after twenty years.

In my dreams I would go back, and walk those rolling pasture hills, lay under the pines, and sit by the creek again. But on the morrow, I would have the stunning opportunity to do it in real life. What would it be like? Would I be ready? Would it be too hard? My mind was racked with anticipation. The next day came, and Angela and I looked at the house. The feeling of joy swept over my soul as my feet touched the 'green, green grass of home.' I fought back the tears. The lady said she would be happy to give me a tour. I said, "That won't be necessary, I know my way around." It's strange how twenty years can change your perception. The house was still remarkably grand. But somehow, it seemed a lot smaller now. The land seemed a little smaller, but it was still so breathtakingly beautiful. The Blue Ridge Mountains were still standing in the backdrop of the Steel Meadow Farm canopy. I began to look at the land and the house like a father or mother would look over a sick child. My eyes started seeing things that needed done, fixed, or changed.

June 25, 2014: Prayer Answered

It has, and always will be, a wonderful experience for me when God answers my prayers. Over my life, I've always had faith that God can, and God will, if it is His will, answer the requests of all those who call upon Him. But in the case of the house, and moving back to Cowpens, was it his will? I just didn't know. The emotional strain and pressure of this decision was so intense, so strong. I had to be right. It would be either something I should do, or it would be the biggest mistake of my life. So much emotion, so many memories, so much sadness, so much joy! I was so nervous. I didn't know any other way than to do what I had always done; "Pray." I began to pray and plead with my Heavenly Father, "Is this your will or is it mine? Is this something that you want me to do? Is this something that can be done?" That night after the tour, I couldn't sleep. So, I got up at 2:00 a.m. and I drove to the old house. I went the back way through Bud Arthur Bridge Road. Coming up the hill at Denton Road, I was listening to Jim Brickman. I was thinking of what God would say to my heart. The answer came! I can still remember the exact spot in the road where I was traveling, and the moment the Holy Ghost spoke with power, conviction, and overwhelming force. I cannot humanly express the love I felt at that moment. The words came into my heart and spoke with my soul. It was so similar to the words found in Paul's epistle to the Romans. The word of the Lord came into my mind saying, "Neither height, nor depth, nor principalities, nor man, can stop the will of the Lord!" At that moment, I burst into tears. I couldn't hold back. I couldn't believe it was actually the will of God! I couldn't believe one of my fondest dreams of moving back "home," was actually something God intended for me to do. Our amazing God was making all of this happen, it was His gift, and He was going to make it happen, not man, not me, but God! It brought me real peace knowing that God was on board with it, and that God was facilitating it as well. He, and only He, could know, could understand, just how much Steel Meadow Farm meant to me. My heart and my mind were ecstatic, but how I was going to pull it off was another thing. How could I make this happen? As I traveled past the house and up highway 110, I was about to go home. I decided to turn around and pull up into the yard of the old house. Its massive profile shone against the black star filled sky. I sat in my truck and just looked at it. I knew it would be a challenge; it would be hard for my family. I knew I would have a price to pay. I felt, and was sure, that God wanted it to happen, so I just needed to have the faith. As I left the house, I drove past Mount Olive Baptist Church. It sits in about 100 acres of peach trees. I can't describe its beauty with the night sky all lit up and shining brightly as I drove past it. The early morning fog was surrounding the church, and the outside lights from the windows made it glow in the dark. I was listening to a song on the radio that came on by Bon Jovi, "Who Says You Can't Go Home." I felt determined to make it happen.

Rich Tyrant wanted me to pay down $10,000 in nonrefundable earnest money and to close within 30 days. This was a very pressing, almost, well, not almost, it was in fact, an impossible task! It was a bad time for the stock market with the economy, and interest rates, being at all-time lows. Everybody was refinancing. Mortgages and banks were backed up because of low interest rates. I had a two-to-three headed dragon to slay.

I had assets, but very little liquid cash. Banks were swamped and overloaded, and I had only a 30 day window in which to work. I began to research people who could help me. Banks, mortgage companies, commercial lenders, and began to be told no/impossible, almost immediately. Mr. Tyrants' wife went to the Cowpens Middle School where she worked, and told the folks there that the house was going back to the Mathis family where it belonged. We began to get calls from people congratulating us, but I wasn't getting anywhere with the banks. It was beginning to look dismal. I started to get stressed and in a state of panic I was trying everything, and nothing was coming together. I began to pray; I began to sing hymns, and was trying to remain positive. I pondered who, what, and how was it all going to be okay, and how was it all going to work out? I was reaching the end of my rope. Coming down to the end of the wire. I was working at an old farm place. The farmer passed away and the relatives were cleaning up and selling all of the scrap metal and junk. I paused momentarily, got off my Bobcat, and walked out across the field. As I walked through the field, my mind caught hold of an image.

Ed Brigman

Ed Brigman had been in real estate for years and years, so I decided to talk to him. I knew if anyone could help me, and give me advice, it was him. I drove to his place and told him of my problem; having assets, but not enough liquid cash. Ed sat in his office chair, leaned back, and he was stove piping cigarettes, one after the other. Every idea I had, he listened to, and rendered his opinion. I saw a change come over Ed's face as I talked to him. His countenance began to glow. He called a lender by the name of Pam Prevett, to try to see if she could help. The answer was long… a repetitive serenade of what everybody else was saying, "Nope not possible!" I left Ed's place that day completely defeated. I felt embarrassed. I felt confused. How could it be God's will, yet not be working out? After that disappointing day I went home. I had such a terrible pounding headache. I was defeated and whipped. I had struck completely out. I told my wife that it didn't look like it was going to happen and apologized for her having to put up with all of the stress. She didn't want to, or wasn't crazy about moving to Cowpens, but she knew how much it meant to me. She said it in a voice of solid gold, and determination, which was rare for her. She said, "You don't apologize to me! I hate it so much for you, but I'm fine, and we'll be fine!" I said, "Well, I'm just going to go to bed and read some scriptures then go to sleep." As I lay in my bed, I thumbed through the Bible and nothing seemed to catch my interest. Nothing seemed to be what God intended me to see that night. As I shuffled through Isaiah, my mind and eyes fixed on chapter 54. I had never completely studied this chapter. If I had, I didn't remember it. But as I read it that night it seemed as if it was intended for me that very night.

Image of Cowpens Brigman Realty sign.

Isaiah Chapter 54

King James Version (KJV)

54 Sing, O barren, thou that didst not bear; break forth into singing, and cry aloud, thou that didst not travail with child: for more are the children of the desolate than the children of the married wife, saith the LORD.

² Enlarge the place of thy tent, and let them stretch forth the curtains of thine habitations: spare not, lengthen thy cords, and strengthen thy stakes;

³ For thou shalt break forth on the right hand and on the left; and thy seed shall inherit the Gentiles, and make the desolate cities to be inhabited.

⁴ Fear not; for thou shalt not be ashamed: neither be thou confounded; for thou shalt not be put to shame: for thou shalt forget the shame of thy youth, and shalt not remember the reproach of thy widowhood any more.

⁵ For thy Maker is thine husband; the LORD of hosts is his name; and thy Redeemer the Holy One of Israel; The God of the whole earth shall he be called.

⁶ For the LORD hath called thee as a woman forsaken and grieved in spirit, and a wife of youth, when thou wast refused, saith thy God.

⁷ For a small moment have I forsaken thee; but with great mercies will I gather thee.

⁸ In a little wrath I hid my face from thee for a moment; but with everlasting kindness will I have mercy on thee, saith the LORD thy Redeemer.

⁹ For this is as the waters of Noah unto me: for as I have sworn that the waters of Noah should no more go over the earth; so have I sworn that I would not be wroth with thee, nor rebuke thee.

¹⁰ For the mountains shall depart, and the hills be removed; but my kindness shall not depart from thee, neither shall the covenant of my peace be removed, saith the LORD that hath mercy on thee.

¹¹ O thou afflicted, tossed with tempest, and not comforted, behold, I will lay thy stones with fair colours, and lay thy foundations with sapphires.

¹² And I will make thy windows of agates, and thy gates of carbuncles, and all thy borders of pleasant stones.

¹³ And all thy children shall be taught of the LORD; and great shall be the peace of thy children.

¹⁴ In righteousness shalt thou be established: thou shalt be far from oppression; for thou shalt not fear: and from terror; for it shall not come near thee.

¹⁵ Behold, they shall surely gather together, but not by me: whosoever shall gather together against thee shall fall for thy sake.

¹⁶ Behold, I have created the smith that bloweth the coals in the fire, and that bringeth forth an instrument for his work; and I have created the waster to destroy.

¹⁷ No weapon that is formed against thee shall prosper; and every tongue that shall rise against thee in judgment thou shalt condemn. This is the heritage of the servants of the LORD, *and their righteousness is of me, saith the* LORD.

King James Version (KJV)
Public Domain

After reading it, I was astounded by its message. How it talked about the reproach of my widowhood, how for a small moment the Lord had hid from me, but with great kindness He would gather me. It said to enlarge the place of thy tent. How my children would be taught of the Lord and great would be the peace of thy children and how no weapon that was formed or fashioned against me would prosper and would be turned against my enemies. This passage, or chapter of scripture, brought me comfort, but I was very weary from the disappointment of the day, and just went to sleep. Later that night, the phone rang. It woke me and my wife up. It was the voice of Ed Brigman. He said, "I've been thinking about your problem, I've talked it over with Jean," his wife, "and Teresa," his daughter, "and we feel in our heart that if anyone deserves that house it's you!" He said, "I've got all my money tied up in property right now, but I do have $100,000 if you need it, if there's any way that it can help." Tears ran down my face as I heard this man offer to lend me that kind of money. It was at that moment, that I realized what that change was, that I saw come over his face, it was

Jean and Ed Brigman

the spirit of the Lord prompting him to help me. It broke my heart to know that he was willing to help. I said, "Ed, I thank you so much, but I honestly don't know, or see how it can help. It won't cover the price of the house, but I can't thank you enough! I'll let you know if I think of anything."

The next morning as I drove to work, I thought about what a truly genuine act of love that was for Ed to offer me money. I thought of the scriptures I had read, and how they seemed to be talking to me. I asked myself, "What is the weapon that is formed against me?" As I thought to myself, I realized the answer was the "money," the "money," was the weapon! Rich wanted to charge me $10,000 just to have an impossible chance of buying the house. Suddenly, I slammed on breaks! I pulled over! I got out of the truck, and looked into the heavens, and said, "Oh thank you, Lord!" You see, the weapon was the money, and now the money could be turned around against Rich, and the banks, both unwilling to help me. I knew the answer! God had given it to me last night in the form of a phone call. I called the realtor for the Tyrants, Steve Metcalf, and said, "Rich wants to charge me $10,000 just to have an impossible chance to purchase this house! He knows I can't do it in 30 days. So why don't we just make it $100,000?" He said, "What do you mean?" I said, "The house can't pass inspection without repairs, and the banks can't close in 30 days, so I'm going to pay $100,000 down, and Rich has to owner finance it for one year. This will allow me to make the repairs, get my house sold, and his mortgage converted to a bank." He said, "What kind of interest?" I said "8.5%" He said, "How fast can you have it?" and I answered, "As soon as the ink dries on his signature." Steve said, "Let me call Rich, and I'll let you know." It wasn't five minutes until the phone rang and the realtor said, "You gotta deal!"

To say I was in shock, would be putting it mildly. To say I was overwhelmed with joy, would be an understatement. After I had done everything under the sun to make the deal happen, I failed. But then, just as God had promised me that night, the promise he placed on my heart came true. It was nothing that I did on my own; it was our Heavenly Father who provided me with the inspiration and the miracle. I know some of the people who read this book will think all of this was just a coincidence, but as it turned out, Mr. Rich Tyrant had taken out a second mortgage on the house to buy some hunting club property. The bank was going to foreclose on the house. The loan he took out was for $100,000, the exact amount that Ed had offered to lend. The day that I bought the house, at the closing table, Rich left the meeting with very little money. First Citizens Bank got 90% of it. I didn't have any knowledge of that situation, but God did. The day we moved in, Rich's wife Ann, sat under a beautiful crepe myrtle tree in the front yard and cried. I felt compassion for her, because I remembered how I felt all those years ago, to have to move. I told her to come back anytime that she needed to. As my workers and I moved the furniture into the house it was apparent that a lot of work needed to be done. It was overwhelming. The color schemes, the wallpaper designs, my wife was not having most of it, "All 80's fashions." That day I got on the lawn mower, and again after 21 years, I was cutting the grass at Steel Meadow Farm, just like I did so many times as a kid, on our Snapper lawn mower. It was a sacred event for me. I finally returned home.

(Thou shalt break forth on the left and the right; thou shalt make desolate cities become inhabited. Isaiah 54:3)

Breaking Forth

Upon moving to Cowpens, things in my life began to heat-up. The pace and strides that I would make are difficult to describe. But nevertheless, I will endeavor to tell this story. Everything happened too fast. Things were coming from the right and left.

It seemed like every aspect of my business, personal, and spiritual life, were being blessed and multiplied. Even our beloved dog, Annabelle, was going through a transformation. There were constant challenges, pressures, and stresses, but we were being greatly blessed, and greatly challenged, as well. Life began to be a roller coaster for all of us at Steel Meadow Farm.

Annabelle

Annabelle was a golden, Heinz 57, retriever/cocker spaniel mix, and heaven only knows what else. She was short, long haired, with a lioness demeanor. She pretty much detested me when we lived at Farm Lake. She was prissy and lay under the shade of a maple tree. She was bored and obnoxious, in her fenced backyard. She liked Angela and the kids but had distain for me, because it was I who always had to get her to the vet, or maybe not. Maybe her feelings were hurt because I never was home. So, we basically, just both tolerated each other.

The day we brought Annabelle to her new home at Steel Meadow Farm, she became a totally different creature. She was completely overwhelmed by the house and the farm. She was afraid of all those crickets singing in the fields. Annabelle completely freaked out over the deer. She barked all night long the first week. It was amazing to watch the transformation that took place with that dog; it was taking place with me, too.

We all felt alive and absolutely free.

Annabelle was a devoted old dog when she came to Steel Meadow Farm. She spent her days in perfect freedom roaming the country-side, playing, chasing squirrels, and rabbits, along with everything else, became her new assignment. She traveled daily to the outskirts of Cowpens. She lived out the rest of her days in complete joy, and yes, we became the best of friends on the farm!

Battle over the Land

The day I bought the house from Rich Tyrant, he promised he would give me a year to buy all of grandpa's 51 acres that I wanted. He wanted to make sure the realtor didn't get a cut out of the deal. So, it was not written on paper at the time I bought the house. Well, that turned out to be the biggest lie that anyone ever told. It wasn't 30 days until he was kicking up For Sale signs on the property. He was trying to obtain plans to build a high density, trailer park right next to our house. He said he could do so because the property didn't have any restrictions on it!

Needless, to say, the war was on! I began again, to panic. How could he be so dishonest? I figured he knew the land meant a lot to me.

He figured I would pay a nice ransom.

Things were about to get ugly.

The first blow came when Rich notified me that he had somehow neglected to include the half-acre parcel that came up to the back of our house. It was on a separate parcel, and I needed to buy it, so no one could build right up against me. Approximately $6,000 was added on to the sticker shock, for less than one half acre of land. The next came when he tried to sell the pasture right next to our house asking $25,000 per acre. So, after careful consideration of what the weapon was again, I realized that it was the land. The land, with no restrictions! So, I asked the same question, again. "How do I turn the weapon against him?"

I just decided to fight fire with fire.

I can still hear the realtor screaming over the phone, as well as Rich, the day I started parking junk trucks, scrap containers, and 55-gallon drums marked with caution tape and chemical warnings right in the front yard at the side where our property joined his. It was hilarious! I added that to the prime property (road frontage) and turned it into a community eyesore in about three hours. Talk about a property value drop! But as I told him, and reminded him what he said to me, "There are no restrictions!"

He was livid. I didn't care. He had caused an all-out war. And with God's help, I intended to win! They tried everything from calling county officials, to lawyers, but it didn't do them any good. They could not make me move the stuff.

The compromise came by me offering to remove the junk, if Rich would allow me to buy a little more road frontage to protect anyone from building right beside me. I said, "I can't afford the entire road frontage, and you want to develop the rest of it anyway." I told him I would let him know how much more land I wanted to buy. I told him that he would have to owner finance it as well, which would enable him to make even more money off the interest! He again said, "How much can you pay down?" I said "$10,000." I didn't know how I could get the money, but I knew I had to try to do something. Rich said he would have to see how much of the land and road frontage I wanted to buy.

Stop Here!

I remember walking through the pasture land, recalling the afternoon adventures my brothers would share on the big rock in the creek. I remembered the times I saw my father in earnest prayer in the bottom land by the spring. I remembered how he wanted so much to build the pond that now I saw before me. The golden memories flooded my mind. As I walked the land, I remembered these precious things of my life, and I pondered and prayed about what I should do. I knew that I was carrying a lot of debt, and I couldn't bite off more than I could chew, because I had to be responsible. My mind raced, my heart pounded, as I struggled with what to do. In my mind, I reached out to my Heavenly Father in prayer, and as I walked, I asked Him to tell me what to do. I asked for His advice. I was so confident He was listening, but I was somewhat taken back by the voice in my mind and heart when I heard the words spoken to me saying, "Stop!" I was walking about a hundred yards back behind the house, heading west across the hill above the pond. I froze in my tracks and thought to myself, "Okay, now what Lord? I have stopped." In my soul, I knew instinctively somehow, that where I stood, was the place where the Lord wanted me to draw the line. As I looked down the hill, I realized that I stood about halfway across the pond. I knew that Rich wanted a lot of money for the land where the pond was located. I knew he wouldn't want to part with it, without being paid a good price. I then looked back up the hill to the east, back toward the house. I thought of how I was trying to get road frontage on the south side to keep someone from building right beside me. I then had the idea to use the place where I stood, the place where I heard the Holy Ghost saying to stop, as a point of origin. I placed a big rock to mark it. I suddenly had the idea to miss the pond by pulling a line from my starting point, toward my left. I used rolls of seatbelt material strapping from an old textile mill tear out, to pull the line from the point on the hill, to the back fence line of the property, missing the pond completely. I then pulled my line from the fixed point on the hill, in a straight line back toward the house and road, in front of the property. The angle that the line took allowed me more road frontage, but angled to miss the pond, and took up on 2/3rds of the wooded, hilly, backside. It allowed me to achieve protection on the road frontage, and decreased the amount of acres I would have to buy, due to its angle. I explained to Rich how the line protected me, and it gave him enough road frontages to develop the remaining property, and have the pond still in its entirety.

He said he would have to think about it. He came back in a few days and wanted to discuss price per acre, per survey. It was an intensive argument with Rich starting the bidding off $10,000 per acre. I would boil-over every time I had to talk to him. I remember hearing how he had bragged about stealing the house and land from my grandpa. He paid approximately $1,000 per acre! Now he wanted $10,000 an acre from me! Just because he was greedy and knew how much I wanted it. I would argue and insult his price. He would argue and insult mine. He knew, that I knew, that I needed to secure some elbow room on that side of the house. And I knew, that he knew, that the odds were in his favor because of my passion for the land.

The mind games were fierce. The emotions ran strong. We both had distain for each other. I would try to appeal to him and give comparable land prices in the area. He would just come back as arrogant, posturing, as to how big of a favor he was doing for me. We finally settled on my price per acre. It was six times what he had paid for it, but I felt it was necessary. We almost came to blows at the closing table. The attorney showed the documents, and at first Rich refused to sign them. He had the closing attorney ready to kill him as well. But, just like with our first deal, he finally succumb to the appeal of the $10,000 cash. Oh, and by the way, the Lord provided the money by way of scrap checks, just in time.

I had no way of knowing the significance of that spot on the knoll where I was prompted to stop. I only knew for sure that I did as I was directed by a source outside of myself. It would take a little while, but in the course of a few months, I would know exactly what the significance was. But in the meantime, I was undergoing a transformation unlike anything I was prepared for. I could not have prepared myself for the storms that were brewing on the horizon of the Steel Meadow Farm. I had no vantage point to be able to culminate and process the facts that would have most likely made me cave in under its weight. But the storms, the trials, the blessings, the tasks, the mountains, and waves were approaching. There would be nothing to save me, only God's mercy and love.

Day of Détente

In the next months that followed, Rich had a land appraiser come out to his remaining property and try to come up with a value for the rest of the land and farm. It was Sammy Floyd, the same guy who first came upon me when I had the bad car wreck. I didn't know about it till some time after the fact. When this appraiser walked the land, he determined that the point where I had been prompted to stop, in fact, established a deficit to the rest of the property. The line established by that mark took away road frontage, a lot of desirable and potential building spots for a development of any kind. In his opinion, the rest of the property needed to be devalued 50% or more. I questioned in my mind how this could be the case, but I guess it all came down to how many housing units could be placed on the remaining property. It made me have a deep and inspiring appreciation for the insight that came into my mind when I heard the word, "Stop."

It wasn't long before I received a call from Rich offering to finance the rest of the farmland to me. We would put all 44 acres together on a separate mortgage. The house remained on a separate note. I cannot express or convey the level of hostility that those next negotiations produced between me and Rich. It was a very bitter campaign. Finally, we settled on $5200 dollars an acre, for the remaining acreage. It brought my grand total paid for the land to $212,000 dollars. A slight increase from the $7000 dollars my Grandfather paid.

Eventually the day came when I decided to sever the ties to Rich by getting the house and land refinanced at First Citizens Bank. I called Rich to get the payoff amounts. I asked him if I paid it off soon would he consider taking less. I figured the thought of him getting a windfall of cash would motivate him to take some off the balance. It did not. I couldn't believe he would sell me property to get small chunks of cash, but would be scoffing at getting paid all at once! It was baffling to me. I would soon find out why he was reluctant to give payoff amounts or negotiate. I once more called Rich to ask for a payoff statement so I could take it to my bank. During the course of this angry conversation, Rich made two statements that brought into light some of the Tyrant's motivations. Rich's dad told him, "You let Steve win, boy!" It made me appreciate the fact that it was all just a game to see how much money I would have to pay for the farm. The second remark he made was also very revealing to me as well. "My wife is mad at me and not speaking." His wife told him, "See, I told you they would pay it off!" It was shocking to hear him admit that they did wish to someday repossess the house and land from me. Finally, the loans were completed, and I got divorced from Rich Tyrant.

It is a horrible thing when love and money leads to bitter conflict. After all, Rich had lived on my family farm for over twenty years. I am sure the place had to mean a little something to him. I don't know; I just know the Steel Meadow Farm meant the world to me. Rich knew this as well, and that is what set the price of the land so incredibly high.

I wish I could have been a better and bigger man when it came to my interaction with Rich. No matter how hard I tried, I couldn't keep a poker face. My face burned red and it was always obvious that I was desperate to get the land back. Looking back, over all those years, I now see myself as a desperate fool who would have paid any price to be back at home. In that regard, I guess I got off cheap.

Health-Tex

I would soon come to appreciate the words in ***Isaiah 54: "Thou shalt make desolate cities become inhabited."*** I am not taking credit for the entire revitalization of my small little town called Cowpens, I can say however, that the first thing I realized on moving back into town was just how run down it had become. It wasn't the town that I remembered as a child. The stores like Potter's Old Country Store, and Martin Drug Store, where my friends and I walked from school on football game days to get a Cherry Coke, were all closed down and boarded up. They had become dilapidated, and the loss of textile and manufacturing jobs had taken their toll on the town. No, I am not claiming in any shape, form, or fashion, to be the savior of Cowpens. But I will just relay in this book, the facts associated with my town and my efforts to revitalize it, and let you, the reader, draw your own conclusions.

After moving to Cowpens, I began to pay close attention to the news stories and articles about a former textile plant called Health-Tex/CNA. It was a very large 230,000 sq. ft. building with 70 plus acres of polluted real estate. The town had been awarded the property by the county when the owners neglected to pay the property taxes. It was a terrible eye sore. The plant sat dormant for twelve years. It had fell victim to every thief and vandal in the country. It was a big, overgrown, dangerous mess. It was not the place you wanted your children to go sneaking into for adventure. It was constantly in the news, suspected of chemical hazards to the community, and its potential ties to cancer clusters in the town. It was such a shame, such a waste. I remember, as a kid, seeing several hundred people working there. I still remember all the cars in the parking lot. How could it now be reduced to this? How could it be so abandoned? How could something with so much potential be sitting vacant? I couldn't wrap my head around it at the time, but I was getting ready to have to!

A few years prior, I talked to the town about all the bad press condemning the unsightly mess and danger that existed at Health-Tex. The town was applying for environmental grants to do remediation at that site. A local realtor, Betty Crocker, was attempting to sell or redevelop the property. I contracted through the town for my company, Specialized Scrap Metal, to clean-up and secure the property. We would bush hog the site, secure all doors, repair fences, lock out all natural gas valves, seal up holes and pits in the floor, junk the abandoned knitting machines on the floor, and we would pay $15,000 cash for the value of all the scrap metal, including the remaining heavy electrical vandalized wire. We would retain the money from all the aluminum, air conditioning duct work, and miscellaneous steel.

Larry Wigington and SSM paid $15,000, and in the course of a month, sold $90,000 out of that mill. We were happy as could be! At the time, I had no idea what a "good job" we had done, junking the Health-Tex plant, but I would come to know in the future just how well we did! As I was saying, I junked the mill and fastened it all up. Betty helped contract the environmental companies and spend all the grant money digging wells to monitor the ground water. Two years or so goes by, and BAM! I'm in Cowpens, back at home, and I have a thought concerning that old mill. I think to myself, "Ah-ha, I could work my scrap metal business out of this old mill. It would be perfect!"

The town had hired, by this time, an old realtor by the name of Jack Newton with Caldwell Banker Cain. I renamed Specialized Scrap Metal to be Viking Recycling. I asked the town about renting me some space in the building so I could operate Viking Recycling Inc. on that property. Mr. Fred Gossett, town administrator, said the town had no interest in renting the building, that they were interested in selling it! So, I called Jack Newton, and said that I wanted to take a look at the building, again. Upon meeting Jack, I discovered that the thieves had wasted little time in coming back to the plant and cutting the locks, kicking in doors, knocking out windows, and stealing anything they could. I still was overwhelmed at the massive size of the building. The ceiling heights were 24 feet in places, and it seemed to go on forever. It was pitch black inside, and as we walked with flashlights, the bats would swoop down toward our flashlights. We walked outside and Jack Newton, the old southern gentleman that he was, took out a chew of tobacco and worked up a big chaw into the inside of his mouth. As we stood there, the old man sat down outside on the steps of the dock area… as he spit a big black and brown patch of spital between his feet, and asked me, "So whatcha gonna give for it?" That question struck fear and excitement in my soul, and raised the flag of possibilities. Here we were, together, two old souls. He, thirty years my former, but now the poker game had begun! I said, "I don't know, I'll have to think about it." He seemed to take my bluff as he said, "How long do you need, boy? I'll take them any offer you wanna make! I can't say what they will take, but just give me a call when you're ready to make your offer." I said, "You bet." As I drove away, I thought about how much potential the building had, but I was so in debt at this point, that it was actually comical. I owed lots of money, and I mean a lot! I was over a million dollars in debt, at this time, with absolutely no credit whatsoever! I was so stressed at the thought of how much I was in debt; the weight was crushing and crowding in on my sleep at night. Every time I woke up at night and thought about it, that was it for sleep! I was working incredible amounts of hours. I would get up at 3 am and work until 8-9 pm. I was burning the candle at both ends, and then some. I could feel the load constantly. I was so afraid of running out of work. My mind was always racing. The years seemed longer, ever turning, and processing every way to make money. I was getting bigger physically, I was still very strong, but I was gaining weight as well.

Now, at this point in my life, how could I even entertain the possibility of buying this plant? But somehow, I felt deep inside that if it was destiny for me to have it, then it was destiny for me to receive it. I had outgrown the White Avenue properties Dexter built and was financing for me. I rode around in the truck and thought a lot about it. I decided in my mind what I would offer the town and how I would present my offer to them.

White Avenue Fab Shop

I decided to use the same old trick that had been working so well for me since my bankruptcy. I would make the offer, by having the town owner-finance the property over time. I would pay something down, and they would owner-finance the rest. The offer I made was in the Herald Journal. It was voted on and approved by the town! The offer was as follows; I would pay $400,000 for Health-Tex, and the property. The town decided they would keep the majority of the acres and only sell me the building and the five acres that it sat on. I would pay $50,000 down, and the town would finance the rest. I had no idea where the $50,000 was coming from, but that's what I offered!

The town council voted, and my offer was approved. They said Fred Gossett made the statement that if anyone could take on a project like that and be successful, it would be me. I will always be thankful for his remark. I made the offer with a 90-day due diligence period. This would give me time to research all the costs of owning such a massive contaminated building. I had to meet with Duke Power, the Waterworks, DHEC, and winter was coming on soon. I needed to be on that site to make my discoveries. The town gave me consent. As I began meeting with the people on site, the Fire Chief, and president of the Cowpens Development Committee, Mr. Caesar Patini, rode by and saw us on the site. He called and asked the town administrator what the hell I was doing out there, and that he wanted me gone. He said that the town's attorney and my attorney needed to run the financials and get the official contract ready. I fought them over it, I already had a contract, and they couldn't interfere with my due diligence period without being in default. I met with Jack Newton at Mike's Café. I was fussing about Caesar's interference, and he said "Well, hell, Steve, you know they are going to sell it to you." He said this laughing, as the cheeseburger grease dripped off of his chin, "The next highest offer was $150,000!" He kept right on eating and laughing, never knowing that he had let the cat out of the bag. I thought to myself, I'm getting ready to pay $250,000 more, plus the interest! I wasn't going for this junk out of Caesar. I told them that if they held up my inspection, I had no choice but to withdraw my offer. That hard-headed little man, with all the authority, wouldn't budge. So, I rescinded my offer and I waited. I figured the math of my generous offer would bring them back to the table; it did not! The local governmental figures and decision makers could not see a good deal when it was right there for the taking. I told Jack Newton to just keep me informed, and that he did. More interested people had begun to make all-cash offers. One of my competitors who had gotten rich stealing from textile plants, and robbing the company he had worked for some twenty years, was making an all-cash offer, as well. It was for $200,000 or there about, it could have been a little higher, I don't know. It seemed like the battle had been lost. I didn't have the money to pay, nor could I borrow any money for an all-cash offer. I was mad and defeated. What to do, and how to make it happen, seemed to be of no use anymore. It was at this time, once again, I would realize the awesome power of a thought! Just an ordinary idea!

"Ideas are the very spark that can create massive fires to brighten our way in dark times. Everything, good or bad, in this life is first conceived with an idea."...SCM

Arial of Health-Tex, Soon to Become Viking

Billy Tobias

I was in deep thought, and licking my wounds over the whole Health-Tex thing, as I drove my old International cab-over truck and scrap trailer, to Auten Warehouses in Woodruff. I was junking some machinery for Milliken. As I circled the parking lot and got my semi-truck into position to back into the dock area, my head hurt, and my blood pressure was up. I hated to lose; especially to Superior Machinery, my competition.

Superior was the company making the all-cash offer to the town. I thought about how it could affect me if Superior got the Health-Tex plant. I wondered what Superior wanted it for. I assumed for warehousing. As my truck and trailer struck the dock, I felt the jolt, and heard the noise, BOOM! I threw the air brakes, and then out of nowhere, an idea! I couldn't believe it! Somehow I had just docked my truck at a place that had a lot to lose if Superior got that much warehouse space. Auten Warehouses Inc. and Mr. Billy Tobias!

I got that crazy, familiar feeling, once again! I knew lightening had just struck in my mind. The Lord had slapped my face, as I hit that dock. It was, "Hello! Wake up! Here you are!"

I hopped out of my truck and made a B-line for the building! I had to tell Billy what was about to happen to us both! Billy, a little fellow, and a great businessman, is in amazing shape. He is full of energy; he has great charisma, and a real zest for life. He is to this day, a cherished friend. At the time I hopped out of my rig and went into the warehouse, we were just business associates. I walked in, feeling like the Duke, big John Wayne. I said, "Well Billy! I got some news for you, and you ain't gonna like it, but I reckon you had better listen up. I just got it straight from the realtor. You know how I was trying to buy Health Tex?" He said, "Yeah I read it in the paper." I said, "Well, the town is about to sell it to Superior Machinery! I figure they will be going after the both of us with the Milliken business now."

Billy, who had climbed off of a forklift, and was now leaning over a box with me as I told him the news, immediately balled his fist up, and slammed it down on the box. He said, "What can we do?" I said, "I don't know, I can fix the building up, but I don't have the money for an all-cash offer!" Billy said, "By God, I do!"

He grabbed my hand and shook it. He looked me in the eyes and said, "Steve, I like you a lot! I know I can trust you. And I would partner up with you in a minute. You make them a higher offer, I got the money, and we will work out the details later!"

I called Fred Gossett and he said the town council was voting on selling the building to Superior that night. I said, "Well, I think I should be allowed to make an all-cash offer." He asked, "How much?" I said, "How much land goes with it?" He said "31 acres." I said, "What about $260,000?" To this he said, "Are you sure you have the money?" I said, "I got the money!" Fred said, "Okay, I'll tell them your bid tonight."

At the meeting, Superior thought I was bluffing, so he didn't raise his offer, and guess what? Yep! You got it right! I got approved that day, by a man I hardly knew, for a loan of $260,000. A friendship developed that will endure this life and the life to come. And, I became the new proud owner of the old Health-Tex building, in Cowpens, South Carolina.

Again, I made headlines with the sale of the building. To say that the building was an enormous challenge was an understatement! I thought I had seen it all by that point, but I hadn't seen anything yet! The challenges of the building made even a fool like me nervous. As it turned out, Billy Tobias had previously made arrangements to sell his building in Woodruff, South Carolina. And again, as it turns out, Betty was the realtor who was representing the property for Billy Tobias. He had multiple warehouses and had decided to sell one of them as we were going to partner up and run the Health-Tex plant. He let Betty talk him into auctioning the building off. I warned him about an absolute auction and told him that I had seen how Betty exhausted the town on the Health-Tex grants. I told him that I would have a fake bid number and would make sure to keep bidding for him until the building had bid what he was willing to take for it. Billy would have none of it. He had his pride and integrity on the line, that it would be sold absolute. I told him he was a fool to trust Betty and that I would be insurance to make sure his warehouse didn't get stolen by bidders working together. He said he would consider it.

The day of the auction came, and Billy regretted not taking my advice. The building brought about half of what he thought it should. It was most regretful. It was a shock to everyone in the real estate business. It also had negative aspects to Billy's net worth. It sold for a low price, which ultimately devalued every warehouse property in the area. It wasn't enough that textile plant after textile plant were closing down, and flooding the market with warehouse space. Now, for the first time, the price per square foot for warehouse sales had set a new low. Billy found out that he could only raise $210,000 of the $260,000 promised to the town. So, I negotiated with the town to hold a $50,000 first mortgage for one year. They gladly accepted, because they were greedy enough to hope that after the $210,000 down payment, they could repossess the building for the $50,000 mortgage. To me it was just a formality, because I knew there was no chance of that happening. The dream was coming true, and I was going to see to it. I felt obligated to Billy as well, to see it through.

Billy Tobias

Thank you, Billy for everything.

I appreciate our friendship.

God Bless you and keep you, always,

Steve Mathis

Sticker Shock

The months flew by. Our due diligence period, and the time too close, was fast approaching. I got a surprise phone call from Billy. It seemed that miraculously Betty Crocker had found a California buyer for his warehouse in Converse, South Carolina. This time, it would be a big payday for the old five-story Converse Mill, that a lot of my ancestors worked in. Billy told me that he was taking the pay day and was going to invest in a golf course and country club down in the eastern Spartanburg/Pacolet area. He said, "Don't worry, I'm still going to finance the building to you, I just don't want to be partners anymore."

I was bewildered. I was trying to keep up mentally with all the rapid changes to these deals. It was like being on the front lines. Bombs were shaking the landscape all around me. Not literally of course, but from a business standpoint, I had never been involved in such volatile changes in positions and attitudes involving real estate dealings. Finally, the day came for the papers to be signed. In the space of a little over thirty days I went from offering the town $400,000 for the building with five acres, having a partner, to not having a partner, and ultimately buying the building with none of my own money for $260,000, and getting an extra 26 acres thrown in to boot! And the scary thing about it all is watching Caesar thinking he has won! I didn't know who had won, but I sure as heck knew it wasn't him. He simply couldn't count! He was a man in charge of spending the entire town's money and selling its property. All I knew was that I went to being over $1,000,000 in debt with a combined 50 acres, to now being $ 1,272,000 in mortgage debt along with 81 acres. The unbelievable thing was that I hadn't spent any of my own money and had no credit whatsoever! I went out to the plant after the closing. It suddenly came very clear to me of what I had signed up for. I had entered into the voluntary clean up contract that the town of Cowpens had signed with SC DHEC before it obtained the title to the property. VCC's are a way for non-responsible parties to assume ownership of contaminated properties without assuming the liability of any environmental clean-up. I just had to sign papers, and enter into covenants to allow DHEC access to the ground water wells etc. I couldn't disturb the soil, and so on, and so forth.

I had a lifelong friend, Joey McElraft, go over to the property with me. The day we walked in, the stench of molded air was very unpleasant. As we walked through the facility, we jumped a vandal on a four wheeler racing through the building in the dark. Every way he tried to escape, we had him cut off. Finally, after running him throughout the building, he found an open door and made his escape. The bats were squeaking, the evidence of burning candles, and Satanic symbols painted on the wall, greeted us everywhere. Windows were knocked out, and the floors were covered in water. Still yet, the building was massive, and I could see its potential.

But how was I going to bring it to life? Where was the money coming from? How could I figure it out? I looked up into the ceiling and all the electrical wires were missing. Knowing that after the vandals compromised the electrical integrity of the building, that I was the very guy who came in and stripped it all out with my deal with the town! I don't know if anyone can imagine the horror I felt knowing that we didn't leave anything to work with.

Talking about shooting yourself in the foot! I had taken a machine gun to mine! Okay, you can stop laughing now. It was a tragedy, but how could I have known, that I was stripping the wire out of a building that I was going to eventually own? I knew the Lord was probably feeling sorry for me, as He was most likely laughing at me, as well! But even then, I was trying my best to wrap my head around this project. The water works engineers came out to the site. They were of absolutely no help, whatsoever. They couldn't tell me anything about how to get started, finding out how the building was supplied, fire protection, versus regular water. All they knew was that I needed a new backflow preventer and meter. DHEC in all its power and brilliance had confiscated all the blue-prints and master plans to the building and had put them in the archives in Columbia. This led me to going to Columbia, digging through the files, only to find that the bulk of the drawings had been misplaced or lost. I would get the most powerful of migraines, as I would walk the floors of the plant looking either up in the ceiling or down at the ground trying to figure out the complex potable water/process water, and fire system water. Machinery, electrical systems, as opposed to the basic utility wiring, all had to be figured out. I would find myself having to sit on the floor and endure the intense brain activity, as my mind raced, trying to remember, strategize, and rationalize the most effective way of bringing the massive monster back to life.

As I write this book, I am reminded, and I see in retrospect, how the Lord God of Heaven was working things out, for my good, on the outside, and even on the sidelines of my life. Things that were happening in the city, county, state, and country, that would have definite impact on me and my business. I couldn't see what was coming, but God knew what was about to happen around every corner, and around every bend. The events, the people, the places, were being directed into my path. All I had to do was just keep working those long hours, exercise faith, and keep looking and listening for the answers.

Entering now into this play, the character who will play a pivotal role in helping me bring the big plant back up and running. A person who would become so much more than just a business associate.

Enter now into the script, Brad Cogdell.

Brad Cogdell and RJ 2006

Brad Cogdell

I have learned that sometimes the greatest blessings of our lives come from first, our willingness to bless the lives of others. It has always amazed me how, in so many cases, the Lord will give you an opportunity to open your heart to others, and you realize that in doing so, friendships and blessings come to you in return. I remember the first time I met Brad Cogdell. I can't remember what I wanted, but I think it had something to do with needing a storm drain for my driveway, or maybe I needed a motor grader to put down some gravel in my shop yard at my welding business in Spartanburg. Jesse Black, my good friend, introduced to me by Joe Garrett, had helped me clear my shop property of the woodlands and such. Jesse had the idea to go around the block on Asheville Highway, to CWG, owned by the one and only, Brad Cogdell.

We went on the property and asked for Brad. We were directed to go up a set of stairs and to the top of the shop area. "Big Brad," was sitting in a setting that was almost like a scene off of the Godfather. We walked into a big dark room, and in the center of the room was a desk with a single yellow bulb dropping from the ceiling, so it only lit up the desk area. There sat a great big, fat, bearded man. I was 6'2, 285 lbs. at that time, and it was hard for me to run up on someone who I felt like was a big man, but Brad was a big dude! He was about 6'2 450 lbs.! He looked like a gangster sitting there in the dark with a pair of sunglasses on! He was smoking a cigarette, and the ashes were dangling about 1.5 inches long. He spoke so smooth and calm. He thought he was the coolest of the cool, the cock of the walk. It was obvious he didn't care if he did any business with us or not. I thought to myself that this guy is flying high on cocaine, or has gone absolutely insane… one or the other. Brad was more interested in bragging to Jesse about the big Home Depot and Wal-Mart site work he was doing than giving our needs any consideration.

I didn't have any desire to do business with Brad; he was way too cocky for me. But I did enjoy the mob boss role he was trying to play. I walked out and told Jesse he was the biggest jerk I had ever ran across and that I hoped I turned out to be that cool when I grew up.

A couple of years later, Brad announced that he was having an auction at his place. It seemed he was getting out of the metal fab business and he was only going to focus on grading and site work. Seeing as I was in the scrap metal business, I felt obliged to go to the auction. This was done in an effort to see what I could buy. The auction was a fiasco. There was junk everywhere! People brought stuff to the site to sell on consignment. At that auction, I bought forklifts for $5 a piece! There were about 50 broken down forklifts. The auctioneer would start the bidding, and then just call my number for $5. I bought about 40 or so of each one. I loaded the forklifts on the truck and took them to the scrap yard to sell for $100 each! As for Brad, well things had changed for Brad. He had encountered some terrible bad luck. He was doing one of those big jobs, and a chain holding a big concrete pipe, broke. When the chain broke, the pipe started to roll across the parking lot. It rolled uncontrollably down into a ditch, and crushed one of Brad's employees to death. What made it worse still was that it was discovered that the employee was an illegal Mexican, undocumented worker. This placed Brad's contracts in jeopardy, and opened up a huge liability for him regarding his worker's compensation. The family of the employee was suing him and his company for wrongful death. Brad was no longer big and invincible. Instead, he had the stress, and look of fear, that I knew all too well, as I recognized it from my own face for many years.

I bought a big metal shear for a cheap price at this auction, as I saw a lot of Brad's equipment and fabrication tools going for pennies on the dollar. I never had the stomach for this kind of auction because it reminded me of how my Dad's was stolen by these auctioneers. After the auction I had a lot of equipment and such to move from CWG. So, I had more opportunities to talk with Brad. Each time we talked, both of us seemed to let our guard down a little more. I could sense that

Brad was as sharp mentally as he was with his smart mouth. It wasn't long before we became comfortable talking and taking jabs at each other as only men folk can do. I began to discover a playful side to Brad. We both kept it well hidden during the day as we conducted business. I offered Brad a chance at hauling and helping me rig the big shear, as I was obligated to move it to Health-Tex. I felt that it would give him a chance to make a little more money for it, and I knew that he had experience hauling it from wherever he had bought it from. We moved the 30,000 lb. machine on a Saturday. I rigged, and lifted it with a 30 ton crane I had bought from Larry Wigington to rig carding machines out of cotton mills.

I had always wanted a crane like the 30 ton Lorain, that I drove home from Mike's café where my dad had last parked it. I had always dreamed of having a metal shear, as opposed to having to torch cut everything by hand. Brad told me he had something he wanted to talk to me about, but that he would come by Monday. I didn't know what he had to discuss, but I told him that I would be right here at Health-Tex. Monday came, and sure enough, so did Brad. I can still see in my mind the way he was fidgeting, and working himself up, to ask me the question: "How much would you charge me to rent a little space here? I won't need much space, just for my tools and stuff…I figure if we can work out a deal, I can work to help you get the plumbing, water, and underground piping straightened out here at the plant."

Brad could hardly stand still waiting for my response. I could tell at this point in his life, he was completely defeated. I could sense this because I had seen it so many times both in my dad's life, and my own life. Brad could not comprehend at first, and then was at a complete loss, as to how to react, when I told him I wouldn't charge him one penny! I told him I would be more than obliged to help him get back on his feet, and I would gladly take his help in solving the Health-Tex piping puzzle. At that precise moment in time, two desperate desperados, became two true brothers, and best friends! I will always remember the tears in two big men's eyes as we shook hands violently, and with such enthusiasm, both extremely happy to have found a friend.

July 24, 2015

Brad and I began to work on getting the water back on at the Health-Tex plant. It was a very complicated task because we had no drawings. It turned out that the plumbing was a closed looped system. This meant the potable water, domestic, and fire protection, all ran together. We started out just trying to get the water on at the office. We got the permits, but we both had different plans. We both argued just to hear ourselves vent! Finally, the day came to turn on the water to the office bathrooms. The meter turned, and turned, and ran, and ran, and finally big Brad came running out of the building screaming, "Turn it off! Turn it off!" That's when we figured out that all the plumbing pipes, both above ground and beneath, were all tied together.

We had water spraying everywhere; sprinkler pipes in the ceilings, pipes running up the wall, everywhere in that 5-acre facility seemed to be spraying water! And so, it began a daily ritual to turn the water on, fix leaks, go turn the water on, shut the water off, fix leaks, repeat. Little by little, the place started drying up. We had enthusiasm about the progress we were making. Brad seemed to be coming out of the depression that had him bogged down. He was working, getting dirty, and fussing with me about how to best tackle each situation. We never could get the water meter to slow down, much less stop. I was looking for underground leaks as I walked out by the 250,000-gallon water tank standing at the back of the plant. To my astonishment, I saw water pouring out of the flange on the standpipe, running up the center. The water tank had supposedly been cut loose from the plant fire protection, but it was now obvious that it wasn't. We got some big wrenches, tightened the flange, and stopped the final leak. We again turned on the water and it turned slowly for days as it pressurized the wet fire protection sprinklers and the water tank. I thought it would never stop. Finally, it did.

Things at this point in my life were coming at me as if I was in a hurricane. Once again me and my devoted crew of Mexicans were coming in at 3 a.m. and working on the building until 7-8 a.m., only to stop that project and begin the work of the day running my scrap metal business. Those were some long, exhausting, hot days. I never felt so strong, so weak, so motivated, so tired, so confident, so scared. Writing about it now, it seems like yesterday, yet, more like a blur. Possibly, like another life. In a lot of ways, I feel like I have lived a lot of different lives. Yet, there is more to tell so I'll just keep writing.

RJ and Joey

About the time I got involved in acquiring Health-Tex, I happened to see two of my old friends from Hoechst; RJ McElraft and his son Joey. I worked shifts as a

RJ McElraft

Joey McElraft

maintenance mechanic with Joey, and RJ worked as an electrician there since 1965. They came over to look at my building and they saw the huge obstacles I faced with trying to occupy it. The electrical had already been stripped out by thieves, and yours truly, years ago, prior to my purchasing the building. The vandals had destroyed the integrity of the electrical grid. I just cleaned it up the rest of the way with my dear friend, Larry Wigington. RJ walked around looking into the ceiling at the entire stripped, empty conduit. Joey and I basically talked about the old days when we were just young pups out at the fiber plant, the people, the people we liked, and the people we didn't. We talked about the hot, nasty jobs we hated to do. Like spin pump shafts, extruder pumps, and turntables, drain pans, etc. The old man

RJ just listened to us, as his eyes carefully took notes. As Joey and RJ were getting ready to leave, I saw him talking privately to Joey. I had no idea what was about to come.

As Joey and I reminisced about the old days, the Spirit of the Lord was resting on RJ. He was a retired electrician. He had worked at Hoechst-Fibers since its construction in the 1960's. Now, it was his time to relax and enjoy his life. Joey came walking back over to where I was standing. He said, "Daddy says he is willing to help you a few hours a day, here and there, to see if he can help you get a little power back on." I couldn't believe my ears. I knew how good RJ was. I knew him as a top notch electrician. I said, "Yes! I would really appreciate that!" So, a plan was formulated that day, and I would have two old friends randomly show up out of nowhere and offer to help. It was another miracle! As I look back all these years later, I realize how God, my Heavenly Father, was in charge of the affairs of my life. I just had to simply show up every day, see what he would provide, and require next.

At the exact time that RJ and Joey showed up to help me rewire Health-Tex, a task that was going to cost between $500,000 and $750,000, it was announced that Milliken had decided to tear down the Gaffney Manufacturing Plant. It was one of Gaffney's oldest and biggest textile plants. A man named Ron Simmons had been given the job to tear down the old mill and recycle the antique brick and heart pine. He called me and wanted to see what I would give for the scrap metal and iron. I asked him if he had a number in mind. I knew it was a treasure of scrap as I had taken all of the machinery out of that building and destroyed it for Roger Milliken. I told Ron that I would come over and look. I hung up the phone and my mind began to race. I was completely stretched thin. I was paying mortgages on the buildings, my house, and the farmland. Where would I get the money? The inspiration came to call Larry Wigington. I told Larry we needed to go look at a job. I told him the details. We went over the next day and the mill was loaded with copper wiring, transformers, and lighting panels, etc. Larry made a suggestion that we would give

Ron Simmons $50,000 for scrap metal rights. Larry would give me the electrical boxes and transformers I needed for Health –Tex, then I would get out of his way and let him have the rest.

I was broke, and I didn't have my half of $50,000 for the deal, so I gladly accepted. We carried the huge Square D, I-Line breaker box down 5 flights of stairs in some cases. They were 200-300 lbs. or more. It was so hot in that now abandoned, dark building. It is tragic seeing the grand ole mill now in the dark. I was glad to be getting the nice electrical stuff that I needed for my building, but I couldn't help but be haunted by the fact that only a year ago, this building was all lit up with hundreds of employees.

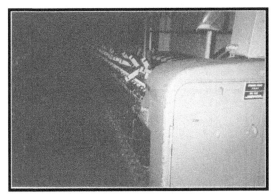

How quickly the darkness came, how quickly the bats and pigeons became the only voices left to be heard, in the huge majestic cotton mill. Constructed in the 1800s, it was as if I could smell the sweat, the cotton, and the heart pine all coming together to smell like the past. My soul hurt for the good folks who lost their jobs. Nevertheless, I kept gathering the electrical equipment I needed to rewire Health-Tex for free; another miracle! Larry went on to gather over a million dollars in copper and scrap. He eventually bargained with Ron to take the whole building down.

Larry became well-off on the deal. I got a free deal on greatly needed electrical equipment!

And so, another chapter began. RJ and Joey would show up, and little by little, the plant began to come to life. It was amazing, just like a huge

Christmas tree, it was starting to light up one bulb at a time. Every big room, or area of the plant we came to, we put another Milliken Square D, I-Line panel. It would be the heart that would provide the power to each separate part of the plant. Things were happening fast, events coming quickly, I couldn't have known what was about to come next... Warehousing.

To RJ and Joey:

You will never know how much your friendship over these years has meant to me. You guys shared these experiences with me as these years have passed so quickly.

Thank you,

Steve

Ken Bolin

Again, I grew up in the Cannons Campground community, until I moved into the farmhouse in Cowpens. I grew up with Kenny and Steve Bolin. They lived at the end of our street. Ken, Sr., and my dad were friends. Ken was an engineer, and executive at Hoechst-Celanese. He later took an engineering management job for Tejin-Monofilament working at the same facility. He was a handsome, intelligent man. What set him apart was his personality and humor. I hadn't seen him in years, until the day he unexpectedly walked through the doors, with no doors, at Health-Tex. I immediately recognized Ken. We shook hands as if we were best friends. We talked about the days at Ivy Park at Cannons Campground. We talked about the Health-Tex/Viking Development building. He wanted to see it, so we took a tour. I told him it was in terrible shape, but he said he didn't care, that he wanted to look. So, we each got a flashlight and began to walk through the building. I can't explain the immediate camaraderie and friendship we felt. I would talk to Ken and tell him stories of the construction, and demolition sort. That first day we stood and talked for what seemed like hours. He would laugh, and laugh, until he would cry and hold his side. He would say, "Oh God, hush!" Then we would both laugh at each other, again. I know this seems bizarre that two grown men would have such an identical sense of humor, but we did, and it was great! At the end of our conversation, Ken said, "I want to lease some of this space to store boxes of monofilament." I told him I was working to secure the building, rewire, and redevelop the property. I told him I hadn't had the thought about leasing space, and that it would take time. He told me what he could pay for rent, and that got my attention. Suddenly, I began to realize the potential that this building had. Ken said, "Listen to me! I need space, and you need money!" I asked, "What do you want out of this deal?" He said, "Space." I knew then, that he was a completely honest man with integrity. Ken began to immediately ship product to my place with no lights and no doors in parts of the massive structure. I didn't realize it fully at the time, but my life was changing. It would never be the same, and God had again, just inspired someone else to help me, and He sent me a new best friend.

Ken came around often as the boxes of monofilament came in, he was all business. He would always smile, wave, and go on his way. He knew if he stopped only for a moment, the conversation would explode into a fit of storytelling and jokes, etc. Joey and RJ continued to make progress, but there was a critical need for wire. I needed electrical wire of all sizes, and lots of it! The building was vast, and miles of wire would be needed. I didn't know how I would come up with the money to purchase what we needed. I managed to get a few runs of wire from Larry, but he was scrapping the wire from the mill as fast as he could pull it out. He could not leave it on the job site after dark because of the thieves. Brad continued to organize his equipment, fix leaks, and do occasional hauling for me. I was even letting him drive my scrap truck to pick up my accounts. Any amount of income seemed to be helpful for him.

Ken Bolin

K-Mart

After several months of work on my building, I ran into an old friend I attended school with. His name is David Hewitt. He told me that he was buying some scrap and junk from a K-Mart that was being torn down as part of a modernization project for the commercial area of Westgate, located in Spartanburg County.

I thought it was hard to believe that the building was being torn down. It was less than 10 years old. Ron Simmons was involved as well. It seemed he had made a deal to purchase the AC units off the roof. David Hewitt introduced me to the foreman of the demolition company taking the building down. They were having a field day junking all the refrigeration units and freezers in the grocery section. They were packing a Ford 350 Dually down with the copper tubing. They kept packing and packing with an excavator until they knocked the whole side of the bed of that truck off! They were getting rich! I told them that I had an interest in buying some of the electrical equipment located in the building. They just looked at me and laughed. See, I drove up in my old white, one-ton panel Chevy truck. It had a cracked windshield and looked like it had been around since the dawn of time. It was so ugly in fact, that Alex and Connor started crying when they saw it! They refused to let me pick them up from school in my truck.

The foreman said I could go look at the electrical room, but to be careful as I made my way through the building. He grinned at his co-workers, as they sat on excavators while ripping out their precious copper tubing. I made my way back to the electrical room, and my eyes about popped out of my head. There it was, "a GE Spectra Series Switchgear!" I smiled when I saw a 5000 KVA transformer, and several more transformers. I immediately knew what was going on. It was all fed from the bottom! All that was coming out of the top of the sub-station piping was small lighting conduit.

Craig on the Lorain Crane at Westgate Mall

It was most likely the reason why the demolition crew had not paid it too much attention. I went back outside of the building and asked the foreman if he would sell me the transformers and the switch gear. He said it would all be gone by tomorrow. He asked what I wanted to pay for it, and I said, "$500 cash." He started to smile again, and I knew that $500 cash was something that he wanted in his pocket. He looked at the muddy parking lot standing in about 1 foot of water where the switchgear was located, he looked at my old ragged truck, and he said, "Pay me! You got till tomorrow morning to get what you can!"

I guess it's true what they say, "You can't judge a book by its cover." They had no idea what I had in my own equipment! There I stood in overalls, welding hat, and my junky truck, looking like I had just climbed out of a trash dumpster. I figure they felt like I couldn't get much out by the deadline. I paid him the cash, and I called my crew, "Load the Toyota forklift, and the Bobcat, on the forty-foot trailer." I called RJ, I told him I needed him, and that it was important. I told my scrap truck driver, Duane Glass, to also be prepared to drop the flatbed and hook up to the van trailer.

That afternoon, I returned to the K-mart-Super K, in the old white Chevy truck. The foreman told me, "Don't touch my copper tubing!" I said, "No sir! I got no intentions of that, no sir!" I waited around and looked stupid, until they knocked off and went home. I had my crew waiting down the street. "Come on boys!" I cannot describe how good it felt as I climbed onto my 15,000 lb. Toyota forklift and crashed right through the front glass of that shopping center! Bulldozing right through the cash register lanes, plowing through the clothes racks, etc., I felt like I was in the wild, wild, west.

I had a lot of work to do before morning! In 15 minutes, I had that big $30,000 transformer loaded on the van trailer. RJ was steady unhooking all the 750 and 500 MCL, wire feeding from the bottom of the switchgear. I brought a snatch block pulley to anchor to the forklift. We would pull the wire out of the floor with the forklift until we forced it to break free. Then we ran it through the pulley right above the conduit coming up out of the floor. I tied it to the old white truck. The old one ton, Chevy, didn't look like much, but it had a 454 big block engine, a 4-speed transmission with a "granny gear." It also had dual wheels with a positive traction rear end. That old girl would growl when I dumped the clutch and began to pull the electrical wire underneath the concrete slab of that K-Mart building. I don't expect everyone who reads this book to grasp what all this means. I will just say we pulled copper wire all night long. My little Mexicans, and RJ, worked like Santa's elves, for it was truly Christmas!

I know God was smiling and laughing watching me work to uncover His blessings. I would pull a run all around the entire building. The K-Mart was located in a shopping mall area. I kept looking, time, and time again, in the rearview mirror. I just knew part of the Westgate area was going to suddenly go dark when the lights went out. It seemed like the copper would never stop coming out of the ground.

My wife Angela called me and said, "It is 4 am! Where are you?" I answered, "Honey, just sit still, I'm not in trouble; no, far from it! I can't leave right now, but I will come home soon." I took a Bobcat, skid steer loader, and dragged the wire back and forth across the parking lot to try and consolidate it; halving the length each time. Then, we would take the 15,000 lb. lift, pick up the folded links of wires, and put them on the 40 ft. trailer.

We came through Spartanburg, after we finished, shortly before sun up. The trailer looked like a float in a parade. Wire piled 4 ft. high, the entire length of the trailer. The tires were pressed flat from the weight of the copper wire that was dragging in the street from both sides of the trailer. I brought the trailer straight to my house. I slept in the next morning. Those guys with the demolition crew no doubt had a fit, passed out, cussed, and probably nearly died, when they finally figured out that a GE Spectra Series feeds from the bottom. I had enough wire to finish Health-Tex and about $100,000 worth of scrap copper to spare. I know now, as I knew then, that God was leading me. He was making the way. I took a picture of my little Mexicans standing on top of the pile of wire, on top of the trailer, and the memory is still etched in my mind. They were smiling like they had just conquered the world, I guess in our minds we had, on a very small scale.

Duane Glass

Kohler

As RJ and I pulled the K-Mart wire through the empty conduit pipes in the ceilings at Health-Tex, the lights were coming on in phases and the plant was taking on a new life. It was amazing to us and we still talk about it to this day. We would pull a run of wire, a couple of hundred feet through the conduit, and we would be astonished by the fact that each time, we only had a few inches to spare. It was as if the wire had been cut exactly for my building!

It was about this time that Billy Tobias called me and said that Kohler Company wanted to lease some space; maybe about 5,000 square feet for a month. He said he had given the purchasing agent my name and my telephone number. Sure enough, they did call. They offered me ten cents a square foot, at a monthly rate, for about 5,000 square feet. That would equal $500 per month! Once again, I began to realize more fully, the warehouse's potential of warehousing other people's stuff. Kohler would truck the showers and bathtubs over and we would unload them. In one month's time 5,000 square feet turned into 50,000 square feet. Things were really coming together!

Neff Bickens with Naggle Lighting wanted to come over and look. He began to find fault with the building. It needed more lighting, etc. I could sense that he was a bad apple, an arrogant, huffy, businessman. I told my friend Billy Tobias that I knew Hubble was his customer, but I didn't trust the guy, and I didn't care if they leased space or not. They declined to lease space, but it wouldn't be the last time I saw Neff Bickens and Naggle Lighting.

Meanwhile, Kohler kept bringing their stuff, and we kept unloading it. It seemed as if it was a season of growth, of harvest. Things were finally looking as if I hadn't made the biggest mistake of my life by buying the old Health-Tex facility. Those were happy days, surrounded by friends. We were thriving, none of us knew, or could have known, the storm clouds were gathering. Miles away, things were brewing on the distant horizon, and it would be bringing its fury while we enjoyed our little moment in the sun.

Spool Cleaning

One day Ken came to me and said, "I'm thinking of moving spool cleaning here." I said, "Okay what do you need?" We looked over the rooms and he decided on a 16,000 square foot room located near the docks. Spool cleaning consisted of people manually cutting monofilament, "fishing line," off of plastic spools. The spools would then be inspected and gauged. This operation allowed Tejin the opportunity to recycle the bad spools, as well as rewind the spools that were still in tolerance. It saved Tejin an incredible amount of money to have this spool cleaning capacity. Ken Bolin and his workers cleaned thousands of spools each week. All of this just added to the space being leased out by my company, Viking Development. This also meant that I got to see Ken every day. We had become close friends. Meanwhile, Kohler was adding more and more space. My businesses were so incredibly busy; it was constant pressure. My body ached all the time, and this I assumed, was due to stress. I didn't seem to have the energy that I once had. For years the doctors had said, "You are depressed. You are getting old. You need to eat right, etc." I was consistently gaining weight. At times I felt incredibly strong, but it was getting more and more difficult to work the long hours.

As I alluded to earlier, it wasn't the last time I would see old Neff Bickens and Naggle Lighting. The day was a sunny, bright, ordinary day when Billy Tobias called me to say Neff and his fellows wanted to come back and take another look at Health-Tex (Viking Development) space. This time, when they came back, they saw close to 100,000 square feet of Kohler product sitting neatly in rows. So, they decided to take the very back room consisting of 38,000 square feet at seventeen cents per square foot, per month. At this meeting, Neff Bickens said, "Hey Steve, have you heard the old American Fast Print is getting auctioned off? You should go buy it! We have a need for space right now." I said, "Yeah I know, I've already looked at it. It needs a roof and it's in bad shape." However, curiosity arose back into my mind as I had toured that property with Jack Newton with Coldwell Banker Cane. He was as tobacco chewing southern gentleman who brokered the deal for me to buy Health-Tex. At the time I had looked at American Fast Print, they were asking in excess of $750,000 for the 364,000 square foot building. Now it was going to be auctioned off. I wondered who my competition in warehousing would be when it was sold. I remembered as a child helping my dad and the mighty SWS crew, put that building together. Perhaps I would go to the auction…

American Fast Print

Noon on Friday, the day of the auction arrived. The auctioneer, Terry Howe, and the owner of the building, Martin Fryml, decided to have the auction offsite at the Marriott at the junction of highway 26 and 85. I had already filed a Freedom of Information form with DHEC, and began to look at the environmental reports regarding this industrial site. Also, a phase one environmental report had been completed, and I was looking at its information as well. I knew whoever bought the building had a lot of environmental concerns to address. Well, once again, I found myself without enough liquid cash. The renovations and improvements at Viking Development were very costly. It seemed like everything I made went right back into the building. The terms of the auctioneer were that a check for $75,000 was due at the end of the auction, and the buyer must close within 30 days. I decided that morning at my office that I wouldn't go. But that morning, as I walked down the hall, I saw a picture of American Fast Print. It was hanging on the wall leading to my office. I had bid on that picture along with a conference table when the machinery and office equipment were auctioned off at the plant's closing, about 5 months prior. I wanted the picture because I remembered that as a young kid I helped make up the bolts, and scrape the mud off of the steel beams that my Dad

American Fast Print Arial

was erecting on that site, as he had put up an addition to it. Somehow, as I looked at that picture, I felt prompted to, "Go!" to the auction. It was that familiar voice saying to me, "Go and see."

As I walked into the Marriott motel, the auctioneer, Terry Howe recognized me and asked, as he laughed at me, "Hey Steve, you come to buy the building, ha, ha, ha?" I said, "Maybe so." I didn't have any money or a check with me! I just felt like I would take a number and hang out and watch. I was dressed in overalls and I had on a camouflage hat. My ragged welding clothes and work boots spelled out to the realtors that I didn't have any money or belong there. Old Jack Newton saw me there and said, "Hey boy, I got you a bid number, I want you to buy it, so I can get a broker's percentage. If you buy it, I done told them you're my customer!" I just said, "Okay sure…" The auctioneers had it all together! Headsets, microphones, coffee bars, and the alcohol bar in full swing in the hotel atrium. After a welcome, some brief announcements, BAMYOW, the gavel struck the wood and the bidding commenced. The auctioneer decided to auction the plant site and 28 acres separate. Then they would auction the remaining, approximately 30 acres, in separate parcels. Then, at the end of the auction they would put the entire property up for sale. It seemed kind of weird, but it's a strategy used to maximize the sale price at an auction. The building first… "What will it be boys? Who will it be boys? "Who will give me one million, one million dollars, who will go $900,000?" The room was full of suspense. No one raised their hand, and the price kept going lower and lower. No one answered, the auctioneer, now red faced and visibly upset, screamed, "Who will give me $1?" Obviously, hands went up, and then we were off. Like an out of body experience, I was having, I can't remember exactly when I raised my hand, but it was some time after the bid reached $100,000, as the bidders had slowed down again. I couldn't believe I was raising my hand. Was I doing it to be funny, or for a joke? I cannot fully explain why I was raising my hand. I was just being compelled to do so. The last time I raised my hand was at $153,000. No one else said a word or made a motion. The auctioneer screamed and yelled at the crowd. "Who; who boys, who?" To no avail, the room fell silent. Finally, as my heart started to beat a little faster, the gavel fell. "SOLD TO MATHIS!" I didn't think much of it. I remember laughing and thinking of the ridiculousness of it. I knew that after the land parcels were auctioned off, that all the property would come back to be auctioned off as a whole. That is when I figured that the big money buyers would start to sound off.

I went out into the lobby, found a chair and went to sleep as the yelling and screaming of the auctioneer sounded with, "Who will bid, who boys who?" I don't exactly remember what I was dreaming about when someone came up to me, slapping me on the shoulder and said, "You did it! Congratulations!" My blood ran cold. It was surreal. I had bid and won a 364,000 square foot warehouse with 28 acres for $153,000! And yet, I realized, really fast, that I was up there bidding with no money! I couldn't even write a bad check, because I didn't bring one of those either! You talk about being in a hot seat; I was. Everybody was looking at me.

The auctioneer said, "Come on, let's get the paperwork started." I said, "Uh, okay… I gotta use the bathroom; I'll be right back…" I needed a plan, and I needed it really, quick. Just then I had a thought! I would call Dexter and Ken, but who to call first? I decided on Ken, because he would know what a good deal it was, and I could offer him a chance to go halves if he could put up the $75,000. I called him and told him what had just happened. I told him I needed his help. He told me that he had his savings in the stock market, and it might take some time. I told him time was the problem, I didn't have any time! He said he would call his banker and call me back. I told him I could call Dexter and he said go ahead, but he would let me know. I hung up the phone. That was strike one! Time for the second swing. I called Dexter Cleveland and I said, "Hey Dexter, I got two things you won't believe… first, I just bought the American Fast Print building for $153,000… he said, "Oh wow!!!" I said "Yeah! The second thing is, "I need $75,000 up here in about five minutes, or I'm going to have to fight, or shoot my way out of this motel!" Dexter said, "I'm on my way, man!" It was like someone punched me in the gut. I couldn't believe he said okay! Five minutes later Ken called and said, "I can get the money and come now." I thanked him so much and I said, "Ken you don't know how much it means to me that you said okay to giving me $75,000, but Dexter is already on his way." I believe Ken was relieved. I told him he could still partner up on this adventure and that made him happy. Dexter Cleveland arrived with a briefcase and out came the checkbook, and the deal was done! Dexter said he might want to be a partner, but he backed out immediately, and was content to get paid 10 percent interest on the money he loaned me. The grand total would be $158,000 including the price of the survey.

I took the rest of the day off to allow it to soak in, grasp the reality, and prepare myself for the drama of owning yet another contaminated warehouse. I told Brad, and he said I was lying. He refused to believe it until I showed him the paperwork. RJ just shook his head and fussed, he once again made his famous statement, "I'm retired!" He wasn't at all excited about helping me rewire yet another plant, two times the size of Health-Tex. People were telling me I was stupid, crazy, and insane to buy the American Fast Print building without a Brown Field Contract. They all said it would be too much liability. It had two waste-water lagoons the size of two football fields.

The water in the lagoons, approximately eight million gallons, had to be constantly monitored. The waste lagoons had hundred horsepower electric motors churning up the sludge, sewage, and water. This was done in an effort to aerate the water volume. Everyone was afraid of those two lagoons! However, I had taken the time and looked at the DHEC files closely. I discovered in the files, that the lagoons had already been drained and the sludge taken to the land field in the early 1980's. I knew a lot of the heavy metals, and VOC's in the ink pigment, most likely had already gone to the land field. I didn't know this for sure, but as I prayed to God for guidance. I felt His reassuring hand on my shoulder. Not physically, but spiritually, that the unseen power was leading me. I had faith that God could show me how to clean the space. I knew He had the power to do it for me, if it was His will.

So, I formed another corporation. "Viking Warehouses Incorporated" was created the day before the closing. Kohler had trucks lined up at the gate the day I closed. They were backed up to the road leading to the interstate. The nature of their foreign manufacturing brought bathroom fixtures from both Mexico and China, nonstop. We immediately began working incredibly long hours. The thieves were so bad, that sometimes we had to stay up all night, just to keep the copper wire we were installing from just being taking back out! All these years later, as I write this book, I am shocked, even though I lived it, to see how incredibly fast my companies grew; how blessed we were. Things were getting bigger, faster, and more hectic. It was all I could do to manage everything. Still yet, inspiration would come to me in the wee hours of the morning or the late moments in the evening, often as I prayed. Sometimes it came as I sat quietly just for a moment to try to catch my breath. I have absolutely no doubt that God was leading me. He was guiding me.

Kohler decided they wanted to move all of their inventory to Fast Print. This came at the same time Naggle Lighting decided they wanted to sign a lease for 180,000 square feet at Health-Tex. We cleared and hauled off over 200 loads of trash, junk, and steel, at American Fast Print. As fast as we could make floor space, more material and product arrived from Kohler and Naggle.

I was thinking one day about the lagoons and the expense it would take to do away with them. In a way that I really can't explain, God impressed plans in my mind, the steps, a plain and simple way to clean up, and to do away with those lagoons. *First*, dewater one lagoon by putting all the water from one into the other. *Second*, get rid of all the water through aeration and the sewer district. *Third*, dry and manage the sludge. I still have the drawing and the plan I submitted to DHEC. They could not believe that I came up with it without the help from an environmental company. Brad and my friend Jesse Black were the contractors who helped me close the lagoons. It took seven years, it was a tremendous undertaking, but with God's help we managed.

Steve is driving. It took 7 years to close down the lagoon.

Storms, Tempests, Broken Deals, and Death

Now comes the part of this book that will take everything I have to relate to you, the reader, and to relive events in my mind. Life can be going your way, only to turn bad, in the blink of an eye. It is at these terrible moments that one must make a choice. Do you forsake God and die? Or do you persevere and trust? Do you continue to take the beating? Do you keep the faith? I can remember every aspect of the terrible times we faced, head on. During this time, I was taking in $98,000 a month in warehouse income. I was spending it all on doing renovations to both American Fast Print and Health-Tex. I was meeting the requirements Naggle Lighting wanted to enter into a multi-year lease. We were working over 90 hours a week on demolition inside the building at American Fast Print. We were building docks, repairing roofs, and closing down the lagoons.

Demolition

Grandmother Mathis

Grandmother, Shirley Mathis, was a small sophisticated woman, and no stranger to hard times. She taught me to love classical music, homemade pimento cheese, and lemon pie. She was a spiritual woman. She introduced me to the Gospel of Jesus Christ.

The phone rang one night after I got home from work. It was my Grandpa. "Son, get over here in a hurry, it's your Grandmother." I jumped into my car and made it there in five minutes. My grandmother lay in the kitchen floor; she had died of a massive heart attack. My grandpa said, "I think she's gone." It broke my heart, after I checked her pulse, to say "Yes, Papa, you are right, she's gone." I got a pillow off the couch and put it under her head. I covered her body with a beautiful shawl. We all gathered around her in the kitchen floor and waited for the undertaker. My grandpa was so upset. He had been fighting multiple myeloma, and bone cancer, for about four years. He had it in his mind that he would die first. It was too much for him to lose his wife of more than 50 years so suddenly. I remember going to the American Fast Print site and lowering the old SWS flag from my dad's business, to half-staff down the flagpole. It was a sign of things to come. I walked into the flower shop in Cowpens and told Pat Sherman that I wanted flowers for my Grandmother's funeral. He started trying to gauge me for the amount of money that I wanted to spend. I told him, "Pat, I want flowers! I want them beautiful, and I want lots of them. She loved flowers and she will have them one more time." Shirley Mathis had a tremendous spray of beautiful orchids and flowers. She had a beautiful service. I put a small quad of scriptures into her hand, and I thought of what a wonderful example of a Latter-Day Saint woman she was. I cannot ever thank her enough for her testimony and courage to challenge my behavior in those early years.

Things were not the same after my Grandmother died. It hurt me to lose her but there was no time to grieve. I had to be strong for my grandpa. I would stop by every evening and check on him. He would ask me about my day and tell me about his chemo and medications. He would always ask me about the kids. He tried to stay busy. Many days he would drive to the barn, sit there, and stare at it. One day I took him for a ride in the golf cart to see a spring I dug out in a small wet spot at the base of a hill. I was trying to find more water for the cows and horses. He said, "I knew there was water there!" He went to take another step and fell face first onto the ground. He couldn't get up. He felt lifeless. He said "Son, when your health is gone, it's gone! I'm so ready to go beyond the veil; I miss your grandmother and Steve." It hurt me to hear him talk like that, but I could tell that it wouldn't be long.

"Dear Grandmother,

I will never forget you and your testimony of Jesus Christ.
The greatest lesson you ever taught me was when
you said, "You can push as hard as you can pull."
It helped me turn my life around."

The Collapse

I thought I had finally broken through to financial freedom and security. All I needed was for Naggle to sign the lease, and the income was guaranteed. I saw less and less of Ken since the American Fast Print acquisition. I often called him to come see the progress we were making. I noticed he was moving a little slower these days. He said his back hurt. He told me he fall rollerblading on the sidewalk. I told him to straighten up and stop acting like a teenager! Within the next few days, I received a phone call from Neff Bickens they had to do some environmental tests to determine if they could sign the lease. I told him there had already been extensive environmental testing at Health-Tex, and that I had the results. It was the first sign of trouble I had with him. After the tests came back okay, he said he wanted a meeting. He let me know that he was paying three times the amount of money for rent at other warehouses. He said, "We are paying by the pallet at our other off site warehouses. You could always raise your rent." I asked him why he was telling me this; did I need to raise the rent? I said that I was only charging by the square foot, and what they stacked was free! Paying by the pallet meant paying by the cubic foot. He also said that I needed fire insurance, with full replacement costs to the building, and it should include an inflation guard. He told me the name of the insurance agent to ask for at the insurance company his wife worked for. It was then, that I realized he was a crook, and was trying to work out a payback scheme for himself. I'm not going to waste time to write all of the details about what happened next, but Neff did not get his kickbacks he needed to sign the my lease. I had already spent over $500,000 making the improvements he requested. I knew I was in trouble. There would be taxes owed on that money.

Naggle Lighting advised me they were going move out. I sued them for negligent representation and for performance of the lease. I had a bad, greedy, lawyer who was telling me I had a good case. I didn't. The case was settled in mediation. The details I cannot disclose. But I did get a settlement. The CFO for Naggle flew down for the mediation hearing. He looked across the table full of lawyers, thieves, and crooks. He said, "Mr. Mathis has what is missing in America these days; a genuine feel for entrepreneurship. I know he has been lied to and misled by my company. I don't care about that. I am just here to see if I can settle the matter. If I find out that his accusations are true concerning my managers, then I will fire them!"

I lost the business because of the crooks. Naggle fired Neff, and other supervisors after the mediation hearing. They knew I was telling the truth about the matter, but it did not matter. We were through doing business. I felt my only hope was to try to sell the American Fast Print building while I still had Kohler leasing the space. Suddenly, I had to slow down the lagoon project and the renovation. With Naggle's departure came a drastic decrease in warehouse revenue. Time seemed to change everything, fast. I was feeling more depressed and run down.

Potter's Store

The day came when I decided I would buy a moped my Uncle Joe had for sale. I'm sure I was a sight, all 360 pounds of me riding around. I had already bought the old middle school I was expelled from. I bought it from Charlie Chan who had it full of textile junk and trash. I thought I could clean it up and make something better of it for the community. It had become a haven for drug addicts and gangs. I cleaned out the building, knocked all the interior classroom walls out using the Bobcat, and turned it into a pretty decent warehouse. I sold it to Kevin Arrowood who made a truck parts warehouse out of it. I thought about how long it had been since I was expelled from that school and went to reform school in the fifth grade.

I looked for more ways to improve my town of Cowpens, South Carolina. It was part of my motivation for taking on the Health-Tex project. The Spartanburg Herald Journal ran a story of me and Viking Development telling of how I had turned around the old Health-Tex facility and leased it to major corporations. It said, "Former Health-Tex facility spends pure profits." They took a picture of me in front of the old SWS sign that had once stood in front of my dad's SWS business. The words, "Why not the Best?" were engraved into the granite stone. Shortly after that article ran, I heard that the old Potter's Store was for sale. I jumped on my moped and rode up to take a look at it. I wanted so much to see it again. I bought candy there as a child. It was an old 1800's nostalgic country store that had fell into dilapidation as it had closed, like so many other businesses during the new Wal-Mart era. I noticed the old corner post, a ten-foot-tall, hand hewn marble pillar, that had once served as a breezeway for buggies to be unloaded, was leaning due to the lentil of bricks failing and pushing it out toward the street. I met with Mr. Ned Potter and the town officials; they wanted to know my intentions for the building. I said, "I want to open up the old Potter's Store." This pleased everyone. The lawyer stated, as we rushed through the closing, that he had never been involved in a hurry up closing, "Before the building fell!" It was in fact funny, but at the same time it was the truth! I began work immediately. I welded up a heavy wall tubing support under the corner of the failing lentil. We pumped ten yards of concrete for the foundation. I then bricked up the failing lentil, and found the whole floor at the back was falling in due to leaks. I took treated lumber I had saved from previous jobs, braced up, and reinforced the floor joist. I bought some old 1x4 heart pine from Larry out of the Gaffney Manufacturing Mill that he was tearing down. It was ironic to me that it was the same age, and the same size, as the one I was removing out of Potter's. We shoveled a twenty yard container of pigeon poop out of the upstairs. I bricked up all the open windows with the solar Coca-Cola style glass bricks that I salvaged from the old middle school. The building took on new life. I bought produce, cheese, hardware, drinks, jars filled with candy, and feed. The wood burning potbelly stove was a favorite hang out in the evening and Saturdays for my lonesome Grandpa, Brad, Ken, Joey, RJ, and Jesse. My grandpa hung out there and talked to Grady Fowler, a friend who was "minding" the store.

Martin Drug Store

At the same time and on the same day I met with Mr. Potter, Austin Dean Shonokee, came running across the street shouting something to me, as I sat on my moped. He said, "Hey, you ain't thinking of buying that old building, are you? I'll sell you mine!" He had inherited the Old Martin Drug store across the street from Potter's. I said, "Okay, I'll come take a look." I remember vividly as a teenager playing junior high football, walking to Martin's drugstore after school, and buying a "Cherry Coke," before our game. The building brought back memories. I didn't know what I would do with it. It needed a lot of work. I thought I would make a teen game room and ice cream shop out of it. I told Mr. Shonokee he had to owner finance it to me for a short length of time. He immediately agreed. So, it was… I bought over half of the main street of Cowpens, South Carolina one summer day riding around on a moped. Both pieces of property had been held by the Martin and Potter families for generations. It seemed strange, but it happened. I was there, and I bought the buildings! Time marched on, as time always does. The teens had a game room at Martin's store. Me, my grandpa, and many friends, had a place at Potter's Old Store to drink a coke or Root Beer from a bottle and fry country ham on the wood stove. I miss those times we shared. Right here, right now, I wish I could go back to then. As I listen to the waves of the sea breaking this morning, I am back in the Old Potter's Store. I can see my friends; I can hear them laugh. The creaking of the rocking chairs on the old heart pine floors, the sound of the tinkling door bells as each one arrived, the smell of that country ham, their smiles, and the light in our eyes as we laughed and shook hands. It is a time, now, forever lost to the past.

A Gold Pocket Watch

I lost my Uncle Robbie that same fall season. He died of a heart attack at his lake house. It was unexpected. He was my mother's sister, Nancy's, husband. He was a general contractor and he loved his family very much. He and Ken Bolin had been friends, as well, as with my dad. It would set the tone for things to come.

It wouldn't be thirty days after his death that I got the news that Ken had fallen and broken a rib that would require surgery. I called to check on him and he tried to laugh it off. I could tell he was worried. After the operation for the rib, the doctors discovered a spot on his lungs that would require further investigation. I will never forget going to the hospital to see him. Ken looked stressed and worried, but he was trying to smile and be upbeat. He told me that he had cancer, but he thought that they could beat it. His beautiful wife Peggy just shook her head, "No," to me when Ken wasn't looking. It was the first time I had ever paid much attention to the word non-small cell carcinoma. My great friend "Kennybop" didn't have very long to live. Maybe if the physician who gave him pain pills for his aches and arthritis had just been able to realize it was something else besides old age, maybe it would have made a difference, but then again maybe not.

I was very upset, and I didn't know what I could do. I found myself wandering aimlessly one day in downtown Spartanburg. I decided to go into an old jewelry shop. As I looked around, I saw an old antique, solid gold, pocket watch. It had a beautiful engraving of an old country home place engraved in the back. In the background you can see a barn, and a dove flying through the air. Its workmanship was fine, its movement smooth. The second hand kept perfect rhythm. Suddenly, I had a thought. I got the jeweler to box it up for me. I bought a beautiful handmade gold chain to attach to the watch. I knew what I had to do.

When I rang the doorbell, Ken came to the door assisted by his son, Steve. Ken looked tired, but he tried to smile. I told him how much I loved him. I told him that he was the one that got me started, that he had put his stuff in my building when I didn't even have all the doors or lights in it! I pulled the watch out of my pocket, and it caught his eye. Gifting a watch came from a time when being a man and keeping your word meant everything. I handed it to Ken. He rubbed his hand over the engraving depicting the old home place. A big smile spread across his face. I choked back tears and a flood of emotion as I said, "Ken, when I was a child in school, I used to look at the clock on the wall praying for the day to pass, for lunch, for recess, to go home. I found that the more I looked at the clock, the more time seemed to stand still. I told Ken to take this watch, wear it, look at it every time you think of it, and I hope and pray that it will do the very same thing for you. I hope it will make time slow down, maybe even stand still." We both fought back tears as he told me that he was very proud of me.

I visited with him a few more times, as my friend Ken was near the end. He had hospice care and a morphine pump. I remember so vividly how it felt the day that Steve Bolin called me to say that it was over. It was just another massive load of grief to add to my spiritual scale. I still often think of Ken. It is so very hard to be at the warehouse, now. The memories overwhelm me. I was very blessed to be friends with Ken Bolin, aka Kennybop.

Thank you, Ken Bolin, for everything.

Thanksgiving

Thanksgiving came around and I was still missing Ken. Change was in the air. It was an election year; would it be Hillary Clinton or Barrack Obama to win the democratic nomination? Grandpa stayed glued to the TV. He thought it would be Hillary. I was concerned about the sudden popularity of Obama. Where did he come from all of the sudden? I couldn't have imagined how it all would turn out, until eight years later!

We had Thanksgiving dinner at our house. My grandpa came over and he was stressed out from yet another round of chemotherapy, yet he was in good spirits. He was dizzy and stumbled around a little bit. He bragged that he had made some sweet potatoes to carry to his two remaining sisters, my aunt Pauline, and Beona. He ate a big meal that day and said how wonderful the day was and he had a great time with the family. He left to take the sweet potatoes to his sisters. As he walked up the sidewalk to their house, he fell down hurting his hand and wrist. He being proud and stubborn, got up off the ground, gave them the sweet potatoes, and went home.

After a few days he started declining. His hand was hurting. After a lot of fuss, he went to the doctor and found out that his hand was broken. Not good for someone fighting bone cancer. He was on a massive amount of medication. Some evenings I would go and talk to him and he would begin to talk to me as if I were my daddy. He would be back somewhere in time. It was very emotional for me to sit there, and to know that he wanted so much to make up with my dad. It hurt me to know that as he looked at me now, he saw my dad! The pain in writing this down is almost unbearable. I didn't try to correct him; I just sat there in the quiet room and let him talk. By the first of December he was weaker. I went to check on him one Sunday because he didn't make it to church, he had messed himself, and I said I would get my friend Troy Williams to come help me clean him up. He reluctantly agreed, but he asked if Troy and I could give him a priesthood blessing. I said, "Of course." After we got him fixed up, he apologized for us having to do it for him. He said, "That's my job." Troy anointed him with a drop of concentrated olive oil. Now, as I laid my hands on my grandpa's head, as an elder holding the priesthood of God, as I am ordained, I blessed him. As I spoke to him through the words of the blessing, I reminded him that this life is a test. I encouraged him to have faith. I spoke through the power of the Spirit. I told him that shortly he would be reunited with my grandmother and my dad. I told him to relax and think of his mother's cornbread and creamed corn, to think of only the good thoughts. I reminded him that he had been blessed in previous blessings to see those that would come for him. I sat there that evening at his bedside as he slept. The feelings that I had are too sacred to write down, but I will say that I was keenly aware that he was ministered to by angels. My grandpa went into the hospital the next day, his blood count was all messed up and the doctors thought that he might have set up gangrene in his hand because it was not healing.

December 14th

While grandpa Thurmon was in the hospital, I was running around trying to keep everything going. I was in negotiations with a California real estate company to buy Fast Print/Viking Warehouses Inc. for 1.67 million dollars. I had my attorney draw up the papers for a no compete clause if they backed out. They wanted to see my tenant rolls, to talk to Kohler, etc. The company was going to hire Brad to be a facilities manager, not only at Viking Warehouses, but at other warehouses as well. It would be a great opportunity for him. It was a couple of weeks prior that Brad and I had discussed his position with them, and he was very excited. Big Brad was a whopper of a man, 6'2" and 450 pounds. He told me that he wanted to talk to me about something. I could tell that he was upset, as tears came to his eyes. He said, "Steve, I know you have four daughters; I am having a hard time letting go of mine. She wants to date and stuff and I just can't get used to it." It was the first time that I saw Brad needing advice, and willing to listen. He usually had all of the answers. I told him that all he could do was love her, trust her, and be there for her.

December 14th began like any other day. It was cool and crisp outside. I saw Brad pull up to the barn and get out of his truck with no coat on. I could tell from a distance that he was about to bust out of those blue jeans he was wearing. He was piping on a cigarette and looking for me. I felt to myself that he needed work with Christmas coming! I didn't have anything for him to do, I felt sorry for him though, and decided I would create something for him to do. I told him to go over to the Viking Warehouses property and pick up his backhoe, and when he got back, he could help me move a storage van body at the barn to a new location. He said it would take him a few hours, but that he would be back around lunchtime. I got on my tractor and began to subsoil the pasture at the farm. It has 44 acres, so it takes me awhile. Brad came back around lunch and we began to move the storage building. I had Juan and some Mexicans picking up debris and moving a pile of bricks. I told Brad that after we finished, he could help them out. Later on, that evening, I hit a big popper tree root in the bottom lands. My TD 75, New Holland was a big powerful tractor. As I hit that big root, it just snatched the subsoil attachment right off the back of the tractor. The root beneath the earth didn't give and tractor didn't either. Obviously, I felt the collision and stopped to look. I was amazed and feeling sad about my subsoiler's demise. I called Brad on the phone and said, "Come down here to the bottoms, I've tore the tractor up." He said okay. When he arrived he was smoking his Marlboro cigarette. As Brad pulled up on his backhoe, I could see he was red faced. He said, "What is it, other than that you've tore your subsoiler up?" I said, "That's it." He looked at me and blew smoke with that red face, and that's when I noticed it was turning bright pink. He said, "Well I've been bitten by some fire ants, and I think I'm going into shock." I guess it was the power of the Holy Ghost who let me see that he was in distress. I asked him, "Can you drive yourself to the barn?" "I think so" he said. I said, "Let's go! I'll take you to the hospital." He took off on the backhoe ahead of me as I climbed back into the cab of my tractor. Brad beat me to the barn. I saw him climb off the backhoe. He took a few steps and started shaking violently. He fell against his lowboy trailer and was struggling to stand up and walk. I jumped off my tractor and ran toward my friend. I saw the face of death on him. I yelled for my Mexicans. I was shaking as I tried to dial 911. Brad tried to say, "Get me to the hospital," as he collapsed and fell underneath the trailer he rolled partially under the truck. Again, I yelled for the Mexicans as they were running to me in a full sprint, in an effort to get to him. I ran to the house, up the hill from the barn. I almost jerked the door off the refrigerator, and turned it over, as my wife screamed! I said, "I need Benadryl, Brad is dying!" I found some Zyrtec allergy medicine and told her to call 911, as well. When I got back to the barn about three-and-a-half minutes had passed. The Mexicans had him in their arms sitting up. He was struggling to breathe. His breaths were shallow. I got him to swallow the allergy meds and called 911, again. "Where are y'all?

Hurry!" I had never seen anything like this. Brad was turning blue and his lips were swelling so huge. I knew his throat was swelling shut. It was as if an unseen force, invisible hands, or a rope was choking him to death. I knew he was going to lose his airway but how could I stop it? I looked around and saw an old water hose lying on the ground. I took an ax out of the back of my truck and chopped off a piece against the bumper of my truck. The hose pipe was small in diameter, and I felt like it could work. I couldn't believe how much his tongue and lips were swelling. As I tried to finger and find his airway, it was all I could do to forcibly find it. As I inserted the tube, I instructed the Mexicans to blow in it every ten seconds, as they did CPR. The light was leaving Brad's eyes. As I ran to the road to flag down the EMS, that had finally arrived, they started using a word called anaphylaxis. They removed the hose pipe, and put an oxygen bag on him as they took over CPR. They couldn't lift him to put him on the stretcher. I had just had elbow surgery to repair torn tendons from lifting heavy steel. I stood over Brad and grabbed his belt and trousers. As I lifted his body, fire shot from my hurt elbow. The EMS people still could not lift him. I yelled to the four of them "Boys, if I can lift his body, surely you can lift his feet and head!" The second time we got him up on the gurney. Brad Cogdell, left my farm barely alive, and we kept him with us the best we could. I got a call ten to twelve minutes later from a paramedic that Brad had coded. They were going to stop at Mary Black Hospital, instead of Spartanburg Regional Medical Center, because his heart had stopped. I went to get Brad's dad, Kenneth, as Angela tried to call his wife. When we got to the hospital we were met by the coroner and the doctor. The doctor explained to me that Brad had gone into anaphylactic shock due to a fire ant bite. When he stood up, and climbed off the back hoe and tried to walk, his blood pressure dropped due to the anaphylactic shock. He went into cardiac arrest. The doctor said that most likely the brain swelling was what killed him. He was amazed that I had the presence of mind to come up with a way to keep his airway open. He said there was nothing else I could have done. It didn't help me much hearing that. How could I have failed in keeping Brad alive? Ken had died less than thirty days ago, and now suddenly, Brad was gone. It was a terrible loss. He left behind his wife and his beloved daughter.

The paper said he was the first documented death in South Carolina from fire ants.

The doctors found only one bite on his hand. After we met with the coroner, I told Brad's wife and family that I would take care of paying his funeral services. I went to the mortuary the next day. I met with Mr. Glenn Miller with Floyd cemeteries and told him that I would be covering the cost of the funeral. It was Brad's wish to be cremated. They had him washed and laying in state for family and friends to see. I was first and all alone. He looked so young and happy. I knew his struggles in this life were over. I told him how very sorry I was that I had failed him. Somehow, I just knew that Brad was flattered and embarrassed by me crying over him. I knew that he and Ken were probably smiling at me and still poking fun. It is so difficult to explain how this private moment with Brad somehow summarizes our friendship. But in this moment, standing with my friend as he lay in state, came the opportunity for me to say things that I should have said when he was alive. Somehow, I believe those same sentiments, were reciprocated by my friend to me. It was only a few minutes that we spent together, alone, but it seemed like a small eternity.

Brad was agnostic, and simply believed that when your time was up, it was up. He felt like everything was a result of, and a victim of, circumstance. In a way, maybe he was right. Perhaps we are all just here on earth, acting and being acted upon. Is it a possibility that everything is just a result of fate and circumstance? If it was not for my faith in Jesus Christ, I believe that I could agree with my friend.

I go back year after year in my mind. I relive that day, and I fight for Brad. I have since placed a big rock boulder to mark the spot where my friend fell that day. I guess it's a way to try and keep him with me. Perhaps it's a reminder of how very fragile this life is. I see it more as a reminder of the weight of my decisions. If I had gone with my first instinct that day, I would have sent Brad home. Would he still be here today if I had, or would a fire ant bite have found him somewhere else that day? It is questions like these that can drive you crazy sometimes. In my most private moments of reflection on the farm I have reached the following conclusion: December 14th 2007 was a beautiful day in South Carolina. It was unusually warm that afternoon, the sun was shining, and the Christmas spirit was in the air. Suddenly, and unexpectedly, Brad's time was up, and his number was called, as he liked to put it. Just like the alarm and calamity of a baby being born, Brad had begun his labor to exit this life. He did this on the farm in the presence of his closest friends. We all faced it together. Death won the battle that day, but the lasting victory belongs to love. The love that we shared for each other remains, and I can still feel it today as I spend time in the fields around the barn. Looking at it all with this perspective, I personally cannot think of a better way to die.

Later that day, I went to the hospital to see Papa. He was lying in the dark hospital room. I spoke to him and he just laid there. He then began to cry. I said, "What's wrong?" He said, "Son, I knew you would pay for that boy's funeral." I said, "Do what?" I could feel my face getting hot. I asked, "Who told you?" He said, "Nobody told me son, I just knew. You got a heart of gold boy, just like your dad." I felt a deep sense of pride hearing him saying that. It was something that I already knew, but it was comforting to hear him say it. I knew then that Grandpa was approaching the veil that separates the living from the dead. The Spirit of God was very strong in the room. I didn't know how much more I could take, and I didn't know how much more he could take.

Brad Cogdell

Brad had a beautiful service. I simply could not believe he was gone. I miss aggravating and arguing with him.

Thank you so much Brad for helping me, as you let me, help you. You were such a dear friend. I couldn't have done it without you. I look forward to seeing you again someday, my friend. Love, Steve

Christmas Eve

Ten days later, I found myself on a Sunday before Christmas Eve, sitting in the hospital with my Grandpa. He talked that day about the farm, his childhood, and his mom's cornbread. He told me the secret to managing grapes. "Keep them cut back, because the grapes only came on the new wood." He would sleep five minutes and be awake for five. He was cycling in and out; he was approaching the end. I told him that evening that I was leaving to take Angela home and told him I was going to have to beat her. It was the same thing that he had always told me about my grandmother, as he would leave from a visit. He smiled and said, "Okay, do a good job," and he tried to laugh. I had been at home about thirty minutes when, right before midnight, just moments before Christmas Eve, Grandpa Thurmond died. I got to the hospital, and he was lying there looking up and to the right of his bedside. I am confident that he saw the angels who were sent to get him.

Papa, thank you so much for your example of hard work, your dedication to the church, your 100% home teaching record, for listening to me, for all your good advice, for your love, and for this spot of ground. I can, and never will forget, those childhood glimpses I caught of you hoeing the watermelons and corn.

I can still feel you here in these fields at Steel Meadow Farm.

Until we meet again, love always, Craig.

My Gethsemane

Two days after Papa died, I had a dream he came and stood by my bed. He was dressed in white, and another man was with him. My grandpa put his hand on my shoulder and said, "Son, I didn't know how tired you were! But I do know now. I can't tell you what's coming, but I can tell you, that it is coming, and if I were you, I would walk away now, and not look back."

I sat up startled in bed! I couldn't walk away from my life, but I somehow knew that things would only get worse. I felt tired, I felt numb, and I felt defeated. I was relieved to know that although it was probably a dream; my Grandpa finally knew how terrible I felt. It was comforting for me to think that someone else knew this besides me.

Breach of Trust

Shortly after Brad died, the California real estate group started to flounder. They used the excuse that they didn't know if they wanted to go forward with the deal without Brad. I knew they were just kicking tires around and stalling me. They had hesitations, it seemed. I told them they could possibly hire me. I told them for the right price I would sell both of my warehouses! After some negotiation, they offered 2.1 million dollars for both buildings. I told them I would work on commission for warehouse space renting. I told them that I would need a car allowance, and they said, "Sure!" I thought, "Wow that was easy!" They said, "What have you got in mind?" I said, "I want a BMW M5!" They said they would go no more than $100,000 for a car allowance, so I started shopping around! Again, I thought I had grabbed the golden ring.

I went straight to the BMW store the day the deal was set in stone. I looked at the M5's, but suddenly, I saw another car that looked sharp. It was an M6! A 500 horsepower, carbon fiber, and all black! I thought man, I deserve this car! I've been driving a junk work truck all of my life. Now it's time to spread my wings and fly, to be an executive, a sales rep. I thought the 2.1 million and the car would set me up good, plus I would get commission! This was going to be great! I was told that the black hard top car was most likely going to be purchased by a Greenville physician that day, so I got out my checkbook and paid $10,000 down. I entered into a three-year, lease/purchase, and it was mine! Now to get that contract signed.

The contract came over via fax. I read it and it looked okay. I had already learned over the years, the importance of reading anything more than once. I laid it down and decided to come back again and read it in thirty minutes. When I got back to read it again, it looked fine. But this time something caught my eye! It stated that they were purchasing both Viking Warehouses Inc. located at Fryml Drive, and

Viking Development LCC located at 276 Foster St. and all its assets! I hadn't noticed it before, because they had included, "all its assets" in the address line. If I had signed that contract, it would have meant that they got everything I owned, not just the two warehouses! Viking Development had other properties including the land and farm. I faxed them back, and I struck out the line that said "all its assets" and initialed it. When I sent the signed contract back with the changes they were furious! They said I had made yet another change, and they were backing out. I called them a bunch of crooks! I said, "Surely you didn't think I was that stupid, did you boys?" So, the deal blew up. I had just lease/purchased a $105,000 BMW M6, and now my "big shot" deal had just blown up, sky high! I wasn't worried though, because I still had the Kohler Business.

Well, as it turned out, the California boys and Mr. Nuetron with Peanut Development had been running a shell game the entire time. They came in talking a big game, going through the motions, shuffling paper and contracts around, while they committed industrial espionage and contract sabotage. They never intended to go through with the purchase, they just wanted my tenants! I made yet another fatal mistake for my company. I had let them talk to my tenants and get the prices they were paying me for rent. The no-compete contract that my attorney had drawn up, and they had signed, wasn't worth the paper it was written on. It said that they wouldn't "initiate contact" with any of my tenants if they didn't go through with the purchase. So, they went to another distribution warehouse, affiliated with Mr. Nuetron. They gave them the pricing info, and they told them that I was in litigation with Naggle Lighting. The second distribution warehouse approached Kohler Company, and they took the business away. In turn, the second distribution center, shipped all of its inventory and tenants to the California Company's warehouse, located in Greer. It was the old Switcharoo! I knew better than to ever let a real estate agent on my property, but I was scared and desperate. I knew I would owe taxes on all that money I spent on acquiring the Naggle lease. So, I effectively, in time, lost all of my tenants at Viking Warehouses!

I kept working alone on my Hitachi 300 excavator, drying the lagoon sludge, piling it high, and letting the sun bake it. As I worked those hot, sweltering days by myself, I thought constantly about how everything had changed so fast. About how so many of my friends and family had passed away. I felt so incredibly alone and defeated. How could I have avoided this? My wife asked me why I just couldn't get along with the big companies. It was a fair question, I suppose. It was one that burned into my very soul. We had about two years of drought during that time, and I piled the sludge high on the west side of the lagoon walls so the summer sun would bake it dry. Then, I moved it and spread it out again. It was a very slow process. I had an environmental company test the sludge, and it proved to be organic material, and had no heavy metals or VOCs! It was a huge break for me! I felt like everything could be alright, I just didn't know how. The county and DHEC gave me permission to land apply the sludge on site. This was another huge break, since it cut down on the cost of closing the lagoons. I sat out in the lagoons running my machine in total defeat and grief. How could it have all gone down in flames so quickly? What could I have done differently? I sat out there and thought of Brad, RJ, Joey, and Jesse, as we had all began the work of closing the lagoons. Now, two-and-a-half years later, it looked like all was lost. Still, I kept working. I was getting more frustrated and tired. Sometimes I felt extremely dizzy, I kept a constant headache, and I thought to myself it must just be because of the constant stress and grief.

Clint Mathis (rear of truck), Derrick Brown, and Rodney Rogers

Easter Bunny

Easter came early that year, and it found my Mama Moore in the hospital with congestive heart failure. She was a very special grandma to us all. There could never be another. She was your best friend, or your worst enemy, and it all depended on how she thought you were behaving. She was no nonsense. Everyone in the family went to see her to get advice whether they actually wanted it, or not. I walked into the hospital with a big bag from the Cracker Barrel. Inside the bag, I had a white rabbit; after all, it was Easter! I gave Mama some small items. I told her that I had brought her the Easter Bunny, and I asked her if she wanted to see him. I will never forget how her blue eyes shown as I pulled that white rabbit out of the bag. After all, the rabbit was alive, and it was in fact, the real Easter Bunny! Her smile took away from the fact that she was now on oxygen. The apparatus was a nose piece that she was wearing. She asked where I got that rabbit, as she petted its soft white fur. I asked her if she wanted me to turn it loose and let the nurses chase it around the hospital floors. She tried to laugh, and said, "You better not!"

As the day progressed, the remaining Moore and Murphy family came by the room to see her. It was good to see her, and her sisters visiting. Each of them have white, snow driven, Irish hair. Later that day she died as my mother sat by her side. My maternal side of the family had lost its anchor. I didn't know when all of the dying would end. My heart was broken. I was tired. The warehouse business was in flames. Time changes everything and everybody. I could feel the heat of the fire. I knew this life was a test, and I knew the test was getting more and more difficult. It was a test I was running out of answers for. I kept my faith in God. I knew the Lord gives, and He takes away. I prayed for strength and wisdom. I knew I needed strength and wisdom, badly, and the Lord was the only one who could give it to me. I didn't know what the future held, and I didn't know if I had a future, anymore. Only time would tell.

Grandma Nell Murphy Moore

Jim Rivers

I developed a friendship over the years with Jim Rivers. He was my contact and a purchasing agent of Milliken and Company. He gave me my start doing in plant tear out and demolition. I would call him or he would call me to schedule the work. By this time, most of Milliken's modernization and demolition work was slowing way down. Sometimes it was months before I would hear from Jim. I would always carry him a Christmas basket, or call and wish him a good holiday. One day, I got Jim on my mind. I called Milliken and talked to Gail Skates Shorter, an old high school friend. She broke the news to me that Jim Rivers had thyroid cancer. He was shaving one day and discovered a lump in his throat. After going to the doctor, it was determined to be cancer and had metastasized, so Jim didn't have long to live. She told me that he had already retired from Milliken, to spend what time he had left with his family. I was so devastated and heartbroken for him. He was a great guy, and a great Christian role model. Again, I just could not believe all of this heartbreak and devastation around me. I called him and I wrote him a couple of times.

Jim died at home about two months later. He had a beautiful service at First Baptist North Spartanburg. I was very impressed to see how his church family loved him, and his family. Jim made a video with his testimony, faith, and newly grown beard on it. They played the video at his funeral. I was greatly moved by it. I knew that once again, God had inspired a great person to give me a break, and to help get me started.

Jim, I will never forget the chance you took on me and my company when you gave me a chance to do work for Milliken and Company. Your generosity and honesty, I will never forget. I appreciate our friendship and the trust we developed. I look forward to seeing you again one day in Heaven.

Your friend, Stephen Craig Mathis

Jim Rivers

Viva la Mexico!
Silvestre Silva Hernandez

After that period of loss and death, the few of us who still remained, tried to carry on and keep the show going. I can say those times were tough and depressing. It seemed as if our entire world had changed so very much. I still had Juan and some other Mexicans working for me helping with the scrap metal business. Juan had become my most trusted employee. He was at work every day and truly appeared to have my back. He came a very long way from the day he showed up at White Avenue begging for a job. I had grown to love Juan like my own son; I trained him and promoted him in my business along the way. He was making very good money during the hay days of my business, and usually worked 80 to 90 hours a week back then.

One day, I decided to take my son, Cross, fox hunting in the woods behind the house. I spotted a big one the afternoon before and wanted Cross to catch a glimpse of the beautiful, elusive creature. While we were hunting, an old man came over to Viking Development and started to look around. He told Juan he wanted to buy some steel. Juan didn't question the man, he just followed his orders. This man told Juan to come and find me to get him some prices for steel. Juan jumped in his truck and came the short distance to Steel Meadow Farm, to see if he could locate me. After he didn't see me, he got back into his truck to return to Viking Development. He pulled out from the four-way stop sign in front of the barn, and a highway patrolman was hiding down the street. The officer pulled him over and said that he did not come to a complete stop. It was a ridiculous accusation because the barn is within 30 feet of the stop sign, and it is a rural area with very little traffic. It turns out that it was Officer Manley, an arrogant, ill-tempered man with nothing but a big ole chip on his shoulder. Officer Manley had to know better, but he charged him anyway.

Well as it turns out, Juan had constantly been caught driving without a driver's license. He had a Florida ID. Usually, he just paid the fine in cash on the spot and went on his merry way. But not this time, Juan was headed to jail.

You see, Juan was already on probation for shooting another Mexican. This all happened the day Juan came home from a hot day on the roof to find his wife and young daughter in tears. His mother-in-law and her boyfriend had been to his house while he was at work, and tried to get money from his wife. When she refused to tell them where Juan kept his cash, they began to get physical with her and slapped their young crying child. Needless to say, that didn't sit too well with Juan. He went to his mother-in-law's house with a rifle. He was met at the door by the boyfriend with his gun! Juan took the man's gun from him when he stuck the barrel out the door. As the man turned to run out the back door of the house, Juan felt it was his duty to shoot him in the butt! I can't blame Juan, but I wished he could have just controlled his emotions. He was just a product of a very hard life back in Mexico.

Juan stayed in jail for over a year while awaiting his trial. At his trial, he was sentenced to five years and ordered to be deported. As it turned out, Juan was just a fake name, and his real name is Silvestre Silva Hernandez. I cannot describe to you how I grieved over the loss of my devoted, little Mexican son. There was nothing I could do to rescue him. I could not imagine how he must have felt to be separated from his wife and family. I worried so much about what he would have to go through in prison. All because Officer Manley decided to shake him down that day on a false charge. Juan was in the wrong, I suppose, well, I guess I know he was. He was an illegal immigrant who made that brave attempt to run for two solid days to get across a treacherous border. He was in a strange country with a new language trying to make money and sent everything he could back to his remaining family in Mexico. I do not think he was given a fair trial. Juan didn't make it any better for himself, as he was scared, and reverted back to speaking only Spanish. I made the trip every year to Ridgeland Correctional Center, near Savannah,

Georgia, for his parole hearings. I would always love and be so full of anticipation to get to see him. I would try so hard in vain to fight back the tears. Juan would always look at me, choking back his emotions, and thinking that I could somehow save or rescue him. I would plead to the parole board to let him go. I would tell them what a noble fellow he truly was. I assured them that I would see to it that Juan stayed on the straight and narrow, if they would have mercy on him. These pleas always fell on deaf ears, and the verdict was always, "Denied." I always looked forward to reading the letters he wrote to me from prison.

Finally, the day came when Juan got released and deported. I was so worried. What would he do? Would he go back home or would he try to sneak back across the border and return to South Carolina? I hoped he didn't lose his life in the attempt, regardless of the choice he made. Sometimes I would lay awake at night trying to imagine where Juan was, and hoped, and pray for him. After about a year, I one day received confirmation that Juan had indeed made it back home to Mexico! I was so happy for him, yet I missed him dearly. I never tried to replace him. I decided to work alone because there could never be another Juan.

"Thank you so very much Silvestre. Your love and devotion to SWS can, and never will be, forgotten. I will never, ever, forget the times we had trying to learn to communicate with each other.
You will always be my friend.
Love always,
PaPa, Patron."

Mystery Solved

After Jim died, I thought about how fast he was taken away. He was in great health; you would have never known he was sick. I thought about the fact that over the years my family doctor always asked if my lymph nodes hurt, and made statements like, "You have a bull neck" etc. Something seemed to hit me this time when I thought about it, and I felt the need to go to the doctor and check it out, again. By this time, I was dizzy. I felt most days like I was standing up in a boat. I ached all over my body. My feet and legs hurt very badly all the time. I was cruising around at about 360 pounds. I walked into the doctor's office and told him that I felt like crap! I told him I just had a friend die from thyroid cancer and I wanted him to examine my neck again and see if my lymph nodes were swollen. I reminded him how he always commented on my "bull neck." As he squeezed my neck to examine me, I could tell by the expression on his face that the light switch had just gone off and things were not good. He said, "I want you to go and get an ultrasound of your neck." I listened to his advice and got an ultrasound. The results came back and showed tumors and nodules in my thyroid gland. My family doctor, Dr. Dorna, referred me to a surgeon. So, twenty years later, I went back to see Dr. Cochran. He was the general surgeon; and the same doctor who saw me in the trauma center all those years ago when I had that terrible car wreck. He explained that I had a tumor the size of a golf ball on one side of my thyroid, and the other side was full of small tumors and nodules. He said I would need to have surgery to have it removed. He also said he would have to do a biopsy to see if it was malignant. He said that there was no way to avoid surgery, and that it was life threatening. He stated there was no way my thyroid was functioning properly.

Suddenly it all started to make sense. I had known something was wrong. The fatigue, the mental confusion, the dizziness, and weight gain, etc. I had talked with my grandpa one morning at Mike's Café before he died. I explained to him all the turmoil with my businesses and such, and that I kind of felt like everything had come full circle in my life. I told him I could no longer see a future for me, and that maybe I was getting ready for my time to be up, perhaps it was time for me to die. He looked at me for a long time and said, "Maybe so, I don't know." Sitting in the surgeon's office, I knew now, what my grandpa meant when he came to me in my dream and said "I didn't really know how tired you were son!" It's never easy to face your own mortality I guess, it's something that everyone would like to put off until tomorrow. Now, it was the big elephant in the room for me. I was so ready to see my Lord and Savior, my Dad, my Grandparents, and my friends, etc. I was also terrified at the thought of leaving my wife and family behind. I was helpless once again to my fate and to all my loved ones as well. Time would only tell what my fate would be.

I sold the Martin Drug store to a young Chinese man who wanted to open a restaurant. I had the thought, that after all, every town needs or has a Chinese restaurant. I closed down the Potter's Old store; I just couldn't bear to go into it anymore. Too many memories and ghosts I suppose. I sold it to a man who wanted to fix it up and run an antique business. The economy was in shambles, my health was gone, and did I have a chance at surviving or would I end up like my friends? So many things ran through my mind. I knew that only God knew and had all the answers concerning my fate. Somewhere in all of this, I began to be ashamed to drive my BMW M6. I realized that it was just vanity to own a car like that, and it was way too fast. Plus, I was way too big to fit in it. I decided that when the lease period was up, I would turn it in and not finish buying it. The day of the surgery came, and I was scared, but confident that I had led the best life I could. Had I made mistakes? "Yes." Was I perfect? "No." But I had made peace with, believed in, and had trusted in God (absolutely). The biggest regret I felt I failed in was not sharing enough time with my wife. I had tried to be the best husband and father I could be, however, I knew I had spent long, incredible hours, at work, and away from her and my kids. I had a big fear in my heart. I told her the night before my surgery I wanted her to be happy. I said, "I know if things do not go well, you will, with no doubt, find another man. I'm not afraid of that, I am just so afraid that you would love him more than me, and I'm so afraid that he would be able to make you happier by being a better man." She told me I was being, "silly, and stop talking like that." It wasn't comforting to me. It wasn't the unknown, it wasn't death, but it was that thought that bothered me the most. I'm haunted by it now, as I write these words. I had a dream before my surgery. I was in a big auditorium. It appeared to be a banquet of some kind. I saw a lot of businessmen. I began to notice some men I had worked with or had business dealings with. They were laughing and talking. Some were feasting at the long tables in the room and the food looked wonderful. Suddenly, I saw Jim Rivers! I ran up to him and busted out crying. I told him that I was so sorry about his cancer. I told him that because of him, I had discovered my tumors. I asked him if they had found his earlier, if it would have made a difference. He looked at me, smiled, and said, "No." He looked so happy, and he said to me, "You will be okay." The nurse came into the room and said to my wife that it was time to say goodbye. I choked back tears and I told Angela to tell my daughter Alex, that if I didn't make it, I would see her at the finish line. She had a state cross country race coming up. The nurse then said "Mr. Mathis, let's go, I got the good stuff in my pocket."

I came to in the recovery room hours later, my neck was hurting badly. I was told that a normal thyroid weighs 10 grams, mine was over 110 grams. It was the equivalent of two softballs having over 200 tumors! The next morning the doctor was shocked to see me standing up and ready to go home. He said, "Mr. Mathis, lie back down and stay a while longer if you want. I had to do a lot of manipulation in your neck to get it out." I didn't appreciate what a lot of manipulation meant until the next day. I was in agony! My thyroid gland, for some unknown reason, had grown up to my ear on the right side, down into my chest almost to my sternum; it had wrapped around my windpipe and was impeding the vascular flow of blood to my brain. Dr. Cochran said my heart was strong enough to pump blood to my brain, but the massive thyroid tissue was constricting my jugular vein. I guess it cleared the air about why I was having some "symptoms" of constantly choking.

The pathology report came back NEGATIVE! It appeared that Jim Rivers had been right, I would be fine! The guess is that somehow radiation caused the thyroid gland to become immortal, to grow wild and out of control. The radiation caused molecular cell abnormalities that resulted in the tumors and nodules. Maybe it came from the X-Ray welding test done on various construction jobs that I had been around, or maybe it came from the nuclear power plants where I had worked. No one knew; all I knew was that I was both thyroid gland and cancer free. I was hopeful things would get better. Only time would tell.

Yo-Yo's and Promises

The California real estate folks would offer again after the economy collapsed, 1.1 million dollars for both of my warehouses. I politely told them not to call me back. I told them they were dishonest thieves, and I would tear down both of the buildings before I sold it for that. It wasn't long before Grise Hunt, a real estate agent with NAI Earl Furman, had an interested buyer for Fast Print. The deal would be 1.6 million. The company buying would be Future Development. I was skeptical, but I had to move forward in an attempt to sell. It would be approximately between four to six months worth of due diligence before closing. It was determined after Naggle and Kohler moved out, that I owed $212,000 in taxes. My ship would have been sunk at that point, except for one thing. During all the time spent at the Naggle Lighting exit, and the Kohler chaos, scrap metal had dropped dramatically during that time, and the market was in upheaval. Gas prices were still very high, and I couldn't understand why metal was so cheap. Something inside me kept saying, "don't sell." So, during that time, I kept piling the metal high. I sold some nonferrous metal such as aluminum and copper, but I held onto the steel for about a nine-and-a-half month period. Now as I faced this huge tax bill, on all the money I spent on the buildings, scrap metal prices came back up. I sold my metal stockpile, and it was just enough to pay the taxes, but the economy still was in decline, banks were failing, big businesses needed federal bail outs, etc. General Motors Corporation went bankrupt. The next year, the taxes I owed would be $100,000, because of the money I made selling the steel to pay for the previous year. I would have to sell one of my warehouses, no other options! So, from that aspect, I hoped that this latest deal would go through.

The contract with Future Development went all the way down to the wire. I was at Ocean Lakes celebrating Thanksgiving when I got the call from Grise. President

Obama gave yet another speech and the stock market immediately fell another 500 points! Future Development investors were pulling out of the deal. The balloon burst and all went away. It seemed like I was in a whirlpool. It was an endless cycle of crooks, swindlers, and charlatans, who would try to put down a little earnest money, tie up the building with a buy sell contract, and to try to flip the property. Or, they simply couldn't get financing. I can't explain the tremendous ups and downs each time I thought I had the property sold, and each time a deal blew up and went south. I began to really be down hearted both literally and figuratively. I felt like I was on an emotional rollercoaster or a Yo-Yo, going back and forth, up and down. Some of the contracts I read myself, and others, I had to have attorneys read. Some would be 50 pages long, filled with boiler plate and legal jargon. I really couldn't believe some of the tricks, deals, and offers, those potential buyers would come up with. I didn't trust anyone. Two events helped me though this time. To me they were supernatural, to the extent that they gave me faith, and it was almost like messages from heaven. It will be my privilege to share them with you.

A Ride to Charlotte

Winter during that year brought some pretty cold nights. The summer was dry and hot, but winter had brought a lot of cold air and precipitation. It was approximately around Christmas time, again. It was on a Saturday morning when I saw a tattered, ill-dressed woman, pushing a shopping buggy along the road in the Spartanburg area. She had on a blue coat and a bright red toboggan. She had several trash bags, and they appeared to be filled with clothes. I could tell she was homeless. She was making her way down Highway 29. I didn't think too much about it until the next day, Sunday, about 10 o'clock a.m., when our family started off to church. We were attending the Spartanburg 1st Ward and our services started at 11 o'clock. As I pulled out from the stop sign on Main Street, at the Old Potter's Store, I saw the homeless woman again going up the sidewalk in Cowpens! I thought to myself as she paused to rest from pushing the shopping cart, "Where is she going?" I drove on to church. The service had started, and I was listening to the opening hymn, the chapel felt nice and cozy. Suddenly, my mind went back to that homeless woman pushing the shopping cart. I thought to myself, "How can I sit here in the warmth when she is out struggling in the cold?" I looked over at my wife and told her to take me home. She dropped me off, and I told her I was going to find the homeless woman. My wife had a class to teach at church and she had to return. She told me to be careful. Opening our garage door, I turned on the light. I cranked up the BMW, M6 that I hardly ever drove anymore. The powerful 500 horsepower engine roared. The beautiful leather seats and the smell of them shouted luxury and comfort. I pulled out of the garage and turned on my CD player to the Jim Brickman CD, "Glory." I drove around the city of Cowpens, but I didn't see her. I drove up Highway 110 toward Highway 85, and she was nowhere to be seen! I thought maybe she had found a shelter, or a ride. I turned around and went back the other way. I decided I would go back to church. Suddenly, out of the corner of my eye, I saw that red toboggan! She was sitting in the parking lot of a trucking company. She looked so tired and lost. I came whizzing up to her in my black BMW and popped the trunk lid. I rolled down the window and said, "Where in the world are you going?" It was the first time that I got to look directly into her face. She had auburn red hair and a face full of freckles. She looked confused, but I could immediately sense her virtue, and honesty. I felt like she might be mentally challenged, but then again maybe it was just from the exposure to the cold temperatures. It would be in the low teens tonight, and the forecast called for snow precipitation. She said, "I'm trying to go to Charlotte, North Carolina!" I said, "Get in!" Again, she looked confused, and I said, "Let's go!" This time she didn't argue, she just struggled to get up off the ground. I helped her up and threw her bags into the trunk. I said, "Young lady do you know how far it is to Charlotte from here?" She said, "No." I answered the question, "Eighty miles!"

As she sat down in the leather seats of my BMW, she audibly moaned a little. The comfort was overwhelming to her cold bones. I had already turned on the heated seats for her. I said, "Why are you going to Charlotte?" She said, "My sister lives there." I asked, "Where are you coming from?" "Myrtle Beach" she replied. "Wow! That's about 300 miles," I said. She said she had been walking for weeks. "I slept last night on the porch of the First Baptist Church in Cowpens." I said, "Are you serious? It was very cold wasn't it?" "Yes," she replied. I couldn't help but to think of how many people must have passed by her, how many folks, including the local police, who had somehow missed her sleeping on the porch of the church last night. I turned up the CD player to listen to the soothing notes of piano music. It had always helped me in the past to put my mind at ease during all the grief, trials, and turmoil. I turned her heated seats up again as the car zoomed onto the interstate. She had never been in a car this nice. I thought of how much she and folks like her deserve to be "riding in style." It made me really contemplate the social injustices that exist within our society, and the homeless. I firmly believe in our free market, capitalistic economy, but there has to be a better way to help so many people who become lost and forgotten.

It wasn't five minutes until she was fast asleep. It was probably the first complete rest she had experienced in quite a while. She had what appeared to be complete trust in me, it seemed. I knew, however, she was completely exhausted. I knew exactly how she felt. I woke her up in downtown Charlotte, and she immediately perked up as she saw the familiar sites. She began to point and name the various places she had worked as a maid or a janitor. She began to direct me down to the suburbs, and finally she said, "Stop! This is my sister's drive." In that moment, she looked at me with such appreciation and love, she said, "Mister, I simply cannot thank you enough!" She then said something that electrified me, "If I had a million dollars, I would give it to you right now!" She continued, "You're a good man, God is going to bless you."

Her words went directly into my soul; they gave me a renewed sense of hope! I knew undeniably that I had been blessed by the mouth of a homeless person. I could not fight back the tears, as I made my way back to the freeway. The sun was setting now on a winter overcast sky. The colors were breathtaking. Later that night, I thought as I went to bed, "Finally, she is home and warm." Today had been a success. I had been able to answer God's assignment given to my heart, in turn, and I had been given a promise. I fearfully thought about her fate, and mine, if I had not followed that prompting. I don't have very much confidence in the fact that I will ever be good enough to go to Heaven. I have made many mistakes in my life. I am depending so heavily on the grace and mercy of my Lord. I know He will do with my soul as He sees fit, and I am okay with it. But this I truly know and believe in my heart: If I do manage to somehow get a glimpse of those who do get to pass through those pearly gates, I am sure I will see some of them pushing those shopping carts, and carrying their belongings in bags. And at that great day, I am certain; my little redheaded friend will turn her red toboggan in for a golden crown.

Will You Be Faithful?

The second event happened about six months later. I was at Ocean Lakes, no doubt working on this book, as I sat along the shore. I had yet another purchase agreement with another company out of Salt Lake City, Utah; Mountain Peak Real Estate. The deal was to buy American Fast Print for 1.2 million dollars. I sat out on the beach while my wife and kids went to the pool. The sunny day was beautiful, and the wind was very choppy and rough. The waves were white capping in secession. It was very turbulent surf. I sat there in my chair watching the waves. I was praying to my Heavenly Father for guidance. I was praying to Him, telling Him I wanted His will to be done. I knew obtaining American Fast Print, was to me, nothing short of a miracle. I just didn't want to do anything to offend God. Was I supposed to sell it? Was it His will for me to keep it? I needed guidance.

As I sat in the sun, I began to think about what God would say to me. I tried to imagine what His counsel would be. I started to get sleepy, I thought about taking a nap, but suddenly the words came to my mind: "You want something from me, but will you watch for what will be lost in the sea?" I thought to myself, "Hmmm I must be going absolutely crazy or the medicine isn't agreeing with me." I really did at times question my sanity! I relaxed back in my chair and thought of the old gospel hymn, "Those in Peril on the Sea."

Then something hit me very strong, I got a sense of alarm, and I thought to myself, "Somebody's going to drown!" I looked out into the angry surf. The waves were way too powerful to enjoy the water. There was a very swift undertow underway. So, I began to keep an eye on the kids and adults I saw getting into the waves.

As the day progressed, I listened to music, pondered on my health, business, and family. I needed so much to have direction, I needed to feel strong again, I needed to know what to do, and I needed to move forward by letting my grief go. But how?

I just didn't know. I needed help from God.

At times during that day, I would walk into the ocean to cool off, and again I would watch for anyone who had signs of danger or stress. Nothing happened. I was relieved! I felt sure that I was just being paranoid. Most likely because of all the trauma in my life, I always looked out for the "what if's", I suppose. As evening approached, I began to think that I would head back to the house and take a nap. As I had this thought, immediately I had the words come to my mind, not to my ears, "Will you be faithful?" I felt electrified, in that moment. It was a second prompting! I decided right then I would sit there until the sun went down if need be.

Around forty-five minutes to an hour before sunset, the sun's hot rays had lost their burn. Most of the crowded beach was now scarce. I looked over the remaining people taking photos and walking their dogs. I didn't pay much attention when a couple walked out to the beach with two small kids. What struck me first was the beard on the young man. The wife had olive skin and looked petite and frail. Then, I noticed the kappa Jewish hat that the young man wore. He sat down and began to read. The wife stood along the shore as the young boys played in the wet sand. I can't recall what I was thinking or daydreaming in my chair when I heard a female voice on my right saying "No, no, come back! Help!" I looked over to find the young couple. The young mom was waving her arms and yelling, "Help me!" Looking back now, I suppose neither parent could probably swim. I cast my eyes toward the ocean and one of the young boys had made the fatal mistake of getting out too far. He was being taken out by the swift undertow! He was trying to swim, but was being hammered by the oncoming white capping waves. I absolutely could not believe that this was happening! Even though I had received the promptings of the Spirit, even though I had been watching and waiting, it was like I couldn't move. Maybe it was because I had sat in the chair for hours or maybe it was the adrenaline, but as I came out of my chair, I couldn't seem to get control of my legs. I almost fell down as I was running. But I kept coming out of the gate just like a horse at the Kentucky Derby. I was running as fast a 350 pound man could, I suppose. I ran till the first wave hit me. I kept kicking and picking my knees up. I knew the next wave would be time for me to dive and start to swim. I absolutely couldn't believe how fast that young boy was getting away. He was now coughing, spitting water, and obviously getting weak. Each new wave came rolling over him and hid him from my view. His little head would pop up a few moments later, and it was very apparent he was drowning. I was swimming full out, my heart was pounding. I was praying, "Please God don't let me lose this race, don't let me fail this boy!" By this point, the kid and I were both fighting to stay up in the huge waves. I believed the next wave that came would be the little boy's last. He was completely out of gas, and so was I.

I will never forget the sound of coughing, and the little boy's faint crying. I was about eight feet from him when the roar of a huge wave broke over the top of us. I can remember vividly being knocked under several feet of turbulent, white water, rushing over my head. Suddenly, in the murky green water below, I saw a lifeless foot come by my face, and I grabbed onto it. Holding onto the foot, I pulled the boy's leg to me, and held on for dear life, as yet, another wave hit us! I had been caught in an undertow once myself, but this one was much stronger. I knew not to fight it, but to swim in the same direction that it was pulling me. By this time, I had the little man's torso in one arm and was trying to swim with the current with the other. I would bob up, lift the boy's head, and hit him in the back, trying to help him cough up water and breathe. I looked toward the shore. It looked like a crowd of 50 or more people were gathered up, and walking down the beach, as I tried to swim through the current and get us back to shore. The little boy's mama was screaming and crying, as finally my foot reached the sandy bottom and I was standing up. Two more guys made it to me, and were helping me stand up, and walk through the surf and rough water. By this time, I heard the most beautiful sound. The little boy was coming around and he was sobbing. I said, "It's okay little dude, I gotcha." He said, "Thank you so much Mister!" and he hugged my neck even tighter. I gave him to his mom as the crowds on the beach clapped and cheered. I was worn out!

Then again, it happened… through tear stained eyes, a young Jewish mother said, "Oh thank you! If I had a million dollars right now, it would be yours!" She hugged and kissed her little boy; the father shook my hand, and then hugged me. I began to try to walk away, when a man I had never seen or met before, walked up to me, and said, "Sir?" I turned around breathing heavily and said, "Yes?" He said, "That was an amazing thing that you just did, that kid would have been gone." I told him in between breaths, "It wasn't me, it was God!" Later that night, I thought about that little family. I thought about what would have happened if I had not been "faithful" to a prompting. I again had the firm and undeniable confirmation that I would be okay, as I was blessed by the mouth of a grateful young mother.

I have often thought about that event. One of my past Bishops, kind of had pause to the experience. He was a very negative person and said, "You have to be careful if you think you are receiving revelations for other people." I just pitied him, and his statement, as he had offended many folks along the way. I'm sure his calling to be bishop came to help him, and not him to help the calling.

After many times of thinking over this event I have come to this conclusion: That day on the beach there were a lot of folks enjoying a day off, vacations, etc. Many were there to relax, and many were there to sunbathe. Some people were playing, people were drinking beer, and some were reading romance novels. I was there sitting in a chair, reading my scriptures, and praying for an answer, as to what God would have me do. You see, our Heavenly Father knows each of us, He knows our thoughts, He knows our tendencies. It might have been at that moment in time, when the undertow was so strong, and the waves so rough, that I was the only one out there praying. Maybe, as I searched for what God wanted me to do; He decided that I could be a lifeguard for Him that day! I guess the odds would have been great for a child to get in trouble that day, and I guess there were lots of folks who could have saved them if they did. But for me, I knew I received two impressions from the Holy Ghost to "Watch." Later that evening, it was only me, a child in trouble, and the good Lord to watch over both of us. I have thought about this event over the years. I thought about what would have happened if I had not exercised faith, waited, and watched. Of this one thing I am sure, I will never win a Heavy Weight title, nor will I ever win an Olympic Gold Medal. But, as long as I live, I will never forget the prize God did allow me to win, as the sight of a lifeless foot came floating past my face in that angry ocean. It was, and will always be, one of my most glorious accomplishments!

Thank you so much Dear Lord, praise be to your Holy Name, Forever. Amen.

My Broken Heart

After I had my thyroid taken out, I began to have heart trouble, immediately. I kept telling the doctors that the thyroid medicine was making me sick and nervous. "Oh no!" they would say, "It's not the thyroid medicine." Time and time again, I would try to explain to various doctors that the medicine was making me very nervous and sick, and again, I would be met with doubt. Thyroid hormone is given and taken in the morning before meals. Normally, you have to wait 45 minutes, to an hour before you eat. When I would get up in the morning and take the hormone, within ten minutes I would get very sick and nauseous. I would break out into a cold/hot sweat, my heart would start to pound, and I felt like every hair on my head was standing up on its end. This overwhelming sick feeling was very debilitating. I found that if I took the medication and went back to bed, I could tolerate it better. I also found that if I remained very still, I could avoid the nausea and dizziness. Throughout the day, things would get better but I would become hypoglycemic if I didn't get even protein for breakfast and lunch. At night I would experience a number of symptoms associated with thyroid disease. The main symptoms were aching bones and fatigue. It seemed that I couldn't build any resistance to the medication, "Synthroid." I can remember and can never forget that day the spring in my coo-coo-clock sprung. I awoke from a short nap on a Sunday morning. I could tell that something wasn't right. It was like a hummingbird flying in my chest. I thought if I could get out of bed and stand up that it would help, but it didn't. It was something that I had never experienced. I tried coughing, and I felt like I should cough but I couldn't. I stepped out onto the carport and tried to walk it off. Bracco, our German Sheppard, looked at me and turned his head sideways, and then his ears stood straight up. I knew my heartbeat was upsetting to him. It was beating so wild and so fast and everywhere all at once. I walked back into the house and told my wife, while trying to catch my breath, that I needed to go to the hospital. It was very hard to breathe, and again I felt like I had a hummingbird was flying erratically around in my chest.

By this time, I was panting like I had just run a marathon. I rolled the window down in the car and laid my head out the window. I kept telling my wife Angela to "Hurry!" I went staggering and falling into the emergency room, "Chest pains," I tried to say. The nurses began immediately to put me on a gurney and take my vitals. My blood pressure was sky high and my heart rate was over 160. I heard a nurse say, "He's in A-Fib with rapid left ventricle response." I hadn't heard any heart lingo and terminology spoken since all those many years ago when I wrecked my car. The adrenaline associated with thinking you are having a heart attack is intense, to say the least. The doctors gave me Lopressor to hopefully calm my heart down. The first dose didn't work; the second dose began to work after about another hour. It was as if my heart had decided to do just exactly what it wanted to do. After my blood pressure and heart rate began to calm down, the doctor said that my heart was beating out of rhythm. They gave me Ativan and scheduled an appointment with a cardiology group. The doctor said they would most likely have to shock my heart back into rhythm.

Later that night after I got home, I stepped into a hot shower. When the water hit the back of my neck and shoulders, I shivered like I have after I have felt an electrical jolt. I began to immediately feel better. I wondered that maybe my heart had jumped back into its normal rhythm. I waited a couple of days for my appointment with the cardiologist. Finally the day came, and I walked into Dr. Ike's office. He had a white coat and blue jeans on. His assistant wired me up for an EKG, Dr. Ike read the tape, and I was indeed back in normal rhythm. I tried to tell him that I thought the Synthroid was causing the arrhythmia and stress on my heart. He promptly ignored me, and said that I wanted to live I needed to start exercising and lose 100 pounds. He whipped out his notepad, and wrote me a prescription for Lopressor and another for Rythmol. I left his office with nothing else to do but to trust him. I can remember the first time I popped a 50 mg Lopressor. I was driving in the traffic in Boiling Springs, South Carolina. I could feel myself gear down when the Lopressor hit me. It felt like I was wearing a cement suit or something. The medicine slowed me down immediately. I felt tired and worn out. The Rythmol just added to the chemical load on my heart. On the one side, my heart was trying to run away from the Synthroid, on the other, my heart was being slowed way down by the other medication. It suddenly became a very hard chore just to live. I had no energy and every moment was lived in suspense, because my heart would constantly flip over into "A-Fib." I would constantly have to lie down and take medicine such as Ativan. I couldn't lose weight because the Rythmol and the Lopressor made it hard to get my heart rate up. I felt so sick, so very depressed. I had completely lost the fire that had once driven me to work super-human hours, and handle monumental stress. My motivation to get up every day was gone. It seemed like my race was already run. I couldn't sense any future for me or my corporations. In a way, I felt dead inside. Each time my heart would go into its own awkward rhythmic fit, I wondered if this would be my last moments on the earth. Every night I would pray to God. I would thank him for another day. I would once again tell him what he already knew. I wanted so much to live, and I wanted so much for His will to be done. He knew the fear I had about leaving my wife and family. I attended church, I read my scriptures, I knew then even as I know now, that God was with me, beside me. He had taken me into his care that fateful day in January 1984, the day my dad got shot. I believe God decided to be there for me, I believe He is truly there for everyone who would allow Him to be. At this very emotionally trying time, I knew that it was only my relationship with my Heavenly Father and His son, Jesus Christ, that gave me any hope; hope to live, courage to die, and the faith to put it all in God's hands. I didn't know what tomorrow had in store, but I knew that God did. It would be according to His perfect plan. I just had to take his advice every day to, "Be still and know that I am God!" Being still was something that I was learning to have to do. I knew in my heart I was at the edge of this life and the next.

Each day I became more symptomatic. I told Dr. Ike I needed to get better that day I saw him. I told him that I had made plans to go hunting Elk in Malaad, Idaho with Troy Williams and my son Cross Mathis. It had been planned for months and I couldn't bear to tell my son we couldn't go. To be honest, I was terrified to go. The thought of being up in the Rocky Mountains about an hour away from civilization with no cell phone service did not sound comforting to a man with heart problems.

The day came that we flew out and I sat beside my son on the plane and I thought about how much he had grown since the time when we rode in my Mack truck, with him in the car seat. Time had really gotten away from me it seemed. When we arrived in Malaad, I was nervous about my medical condition, but I was anxious for Cross to see the sunrises and the sunsets along the tops of the Rocky Mountains. I wanted him to see the breathtaking night time skies as each star would shine so clearly, to hear the wolves and the coyotes that would cry and howl at the approaching moon, and yes of course, to hear the mighty elk, as the bulls began to fight and blow the mating calls of the fall.

Base camp was beautiful as always, nestled back up against a mountain ravine with the white bark of the Aspen trees, saying to one's soul, "Welcome to the Rockies!" Troy's brothers, Doyle and Rex, were there, as well as Heffer, our cook. My guide's name was Hubbard. It was exciting to see Cross engrave his initials into the big Aspen tree. It was an annual event to carve and tear your name into the soft white bark. Each morning we would climb to the top of the Rockies and try to "glass" the elk grazing in the alfalfa fields below, and it was so very hard to climb those trails. I would lag behind the others, panting and trying to breathe, in the high altitude. The Lopressor and the Rythmol didn't help either. After a couple of days at camp, Cross and I decided to go on an evening hunt alone. I decided that we would go to Don's Pocket; it was a place that I had missed the opportunity to kill a 5x5 elk the previous year. It was an absolutely gorgeous view. We would have the sun at our back and the moon would appear above the sky below. When we got there, we got set up for the elk. I hoped that if the elk didn't show at least one of the huge mule deer would. We had been there a while, and it was so picturesque. I really loved the feeling of bow hunting with my son. As the evening shadows fell, I knew it would be wise to head back to camp. I told Cross that we needed to go; it was at that moment that I realized I couldn't feel anything below my right hip. I tried to stand up, and as I did I couldn't feel anything. I tried to put weight on my leg and walk and I almost fell. I couldn't move my right leg, it was paralyzed. Fear and terror once again started to overcome me, "Was I having a stroke? What if I fell and broke my hip trying to hike back to the 4x4's?" I knew Cross didn't know the way back to camp. I just prayed to God to help me in this moment with all my might. It took about twenty minutes of shaking my leg and standing up to finally regain the feeling in my leg. Eventually, I was able to walk. After we made it back to camp, I had to break the news to my son that we would have to go down off the mountain and go back to Salt Lake in the morning. I wanted to be safe and I wanted to have him with me in the event that I had to go to the hospital or the ER. He was as disappointed as any 14 year old could be. But he agreed and was a fine gentleman about it all. We took the rental car off the mountain and found a hotel close to Salt Lake. I felt a lot better being near the hospital for the remainder of our trip.

Cross and I made the most of it. God helped us to be blessed, even though we weren't able to chase the elk. I took him to see the Missionary Training Center in Provo, Utah, (MTC), and it was filled with missionaries for The Church of Jesus Christ of Latter-Day Saints. We got to see the thousands of young people preparing to go on missions all over the world. I took him to see the campus, and the football stadium at BYU. Our most amazing time came as we saw the LDS convention center. I wanted to let Cross get a look through the door. Instead we were greeted by the missionaries and they gave us the full tour. We saw the park on top of the convention center, all the original paintings of Christ and the prophets. They told us to come back in the morning and we could see "Music in the Spoken Word," live. What an awesome event and chance to see the Mormon Tabernacle Choir live. We visited a local target and we got some casual clothes, as we had only brought camouflage. We were excited. The next morning, we got there early, we got good seats, and finally it was time to see the show. It was breathtaking hearing the Mormon Tabernacle Choir sing, the Spirit of God was very strong. It was an experience we will never forget.

We soon made our way back home on the Southwest jet. I knew I needed to go back to see Dr. Ike. I no sooner got home that I had another attack. I took my medicine, and as soon as I did it felt like I had swallowed a basketball, I couldn't get my breath. I called the emergency hotline to the cardiology group; the doctor on call told me to stop taking the Rythmol and go straight the ER. I got to the ER and my heart rate was in the mid 30's. I was close to having heart failure. The doctors made adjustments to my medication, and I was to stop taking Rythmol, all together. It was to be an ongoing struggle to somehow find cardiac balance for me.

Cross and Steve in Idaho

The Gun

About a year after the sale of Potter's Old Store, I was contacted by Chris Potter. His dad, Ned Potter, had sold me the old store. I believe he asked me on Facebook if I still had the old black safe that came out of the old store. I told him that I collected old safes, and that I indeed had kept it. He asked what I would sell it for. He said, "My son would like to refurbish it and keep it in the family." I told him I would think about it and let him know. His next statement made me stop dead in my tracks! My blood ran cold, and my mind went completely blank!

He said, "I got the gun, you know …what happened…. to your dad." I questioned in my mind the truthfulness of his statement. My grandpa had told us for years that he gave it to the sheriff's department to destroy it. How could after all these years, the story change? Was it possible? I asked him if he was sure he knew what he was talking about? He said, "Yes, Pat Bishop had bought the gun from my Papa. He kept it put away until he sold all his guns to Ned Potter." Ned told Chris that this was the gun, a nickel plated, Colt Diamondback, 38 Special. Chris said, "I'll trade you the gun for the safe." It was awkward to hear myself say the words, "Okay." I didn't want "the gun," but I didn't want anyone else having bragging rights to owning it either.

With all the power of my soul, I can't express the weight of that gun when I took it from Chris' hand. I don't know to this day how I kept my emotions in check, it was very difficult. I delivered the old black Potter's Store safe to Mrs. Shirley Potter, Chris' mom, and his son restored it back to its original condition. As for the gun, well it set off a series of emotions and questions as it took me back in time to the day the phone rang, and I heard my mother scream. Oh, how did it happen?

Why did it happen? And why, oh why, did the gun make its way, 31 years later, back into my hands? Why? I had to find out!

"The gun" was wrapped in a white linen cloth, and I have no doubt that was what my grandpa wrapped it in so very long ago. "The gun" reminded me of a body in a burial shroud; it was in fact, what ended my father's life. "The gun" altered my life in a terrible way. And, "the gun" set me off on a journey back in time, once more. As I write these words, my mind's eyes, and my natural eyes, are filled with tears. The return of this gun would ultimately be a "key" of sorts, a key that would unlock a door, and a key that would take me back to see through the eyes of a mature man, and back to the events of my eighteenth birthday. I would go back and relive it all again. I didn't know it at the time, but "the gun" would do all of this.

I wrote the serial number of "the gun" down and I locked it in my safe. I contacted a childhood friend, a police officer, Doug Whitaker. I asked him how to go about looking up the police report and coroner's report filed on my dad's shooting. He said I could contact the Cherokee County Coroner's Office to obtain the report. He said he would look into the police report. I told him I remembered that only one fingerprint, "a partial print," was found on "the gun." I asked him if the new aurora technology could match that partial print. We both agreed and thought it could be a possibility. These questions would start a very frustrating series of events as I tried so hard to obtain information over three decades old.

The coroner's report was extensive, it did confirm that the serial number of "the gun" I had now, was indeed "the gun" that killed my father. I don't know why my grandpa lied about having it destroyed; perhaps it was an effort to prevent what was happening right now at this very moment in my life! There was something very odd to me about this gun; it looked more like a gun a woman would carry. My dad was an expert marksman; he was proficient, as am I, with the 1911 model, forty-five caliber automatic pistols. He liked the Rugger, Super Black Hawk, Cowboy gun "three screws." I didn't remember ever seeing this Colt Diamondback, as a kid, in my father's possession. My gut instinct told me it wasn't something he would carry. Again, I wrote down the serial number and typed a letter to Colt Firearms archive department. I mailed Colt the money required to attain the history on "the gun."

I received Colt Firearms' correspondence telling me it would take three months before they could send me the letter of origin. Doug Whitaker informed me the police records of my dad's death were lost when the police department flooded ten years ago. I contacted SLED (South Carolina Law Enforcement Division). SLED was the agency that did the ballistics test on the pieces of fragmented bullets to determine that the bullets came from the Colt Diamondback. SLED informed me that they no longer had that evidence! I couldn't believe what I was hearing!

The police reports were gone! The SLED evidence was gone! Something didn't seem right! Then, the incredible happened! I went to the hospital to try and get my father's medical records. I told them he had been deceased since 1984, and I wanted his medical records to compare to my ill health. I felt like that sounded better than saying I was looking into the events of his homicide. The records department then asked if I was his power of attorney, I said no, that my grandfather was, and that he had been deceased now for about five years. The lady at the records department said I would have to go to the probate office of the county courthouse to reopen his case, and I would have to call for an appointment. I called the probate office and made an appointment. It would take three more weeks!

Finally, the day came. I was told at the meeting that my mother, two brothers, Clint, and Clay would have to sign a form, naming me the executor of the reopened file of "Stephen Terry Mathis." Somehow, miraculously, they all signed the document without putting up much of a fuss. I wasn't worried about my mother signing it, but I didn't know how my brothers would react. It wasn't a pleasant thing for any of us to deal with again. Nevertheless, I took the form back to the probate office and they gave me the letter of being the authorized agent. I took the form back to the hospital and gave the letter to the records office. After they confirmed my information, they proceeded to look for the information requested.

The lady returned shortly and said, "I'm sorry, there are no records for Stephen Terry Mathis!" I couldn't believe what I was hearing her say; I had been waiting weeks for this information. Now, I was being told "no records!" I said, "M'am let me explain something to you! I was an eighteen-year-old boy when my dad was brought into this hospital on January 16, 1984 for a gunshot wound to the head. He was operated on here, and he lived here for approximately two weeks until he passed away on Sunday, February 5, 1984. I know! I was here! Now, I have a copy of the coroner's report and the death certificate that also says he was here! It is absolutely beyond bizarre and totally unacceptable for you to stand here and say there are no records! I want them found, and I want it now! I will not go away! If I have to sue this hospital, I will. Someone will find these records!" She stared at me for a moment and said, "I'll have to go see my supervisor." I said, "Go see whoever it takes." After several minutes, she returned with her supervisor. I was told the records were not there, but they might have somewhere else they could look. I was promised I would be contacted in a day or so.

Finally, after two or three days, I received a call from the records department. They said they had found my dad's records after searching in "other areas." She said some were hard copied, some were microfilmed, and it would take time to get them for me. She said it could be expensive. I promptly told her that I didn't care, copy them, and let me know when they were ready. Meanwhile, I reached out and asked both Doug Whitaker and Detective Doug Smith to look over the transcript of the proceedings at the coroner's inquest. I acquired a copy of it with the coroner's report; it was the account of what happened on the evening of January 16, 1984, according to various witness statements.

I couldn't believe, now as a man, the details of what I read, or the statements given. Everything was botched. "The gun" which was across the hall from my father's room, was touched by numerous people, "detectives," yet only one partial print was found! It was obvious the gun had been wiped clean. My dad had been shot in the back of the head, the bullet traveling at a downward angle. There was no (GSR) gunshot residue test done on my father nor on Miss Harris, who claimed to be there at the shooting. No statements were even taken the day of the shooting. People came to the sheriff's office later, some even days later, to give statements. Nothing added up.

My dad had multiple guns and pistols in his apartment, the other guns were recovered at the scene. It was the most horrific case of sloppy police work I had ever seen, or heard tell of. It seemed as if the police themselves were involved in a cover up.

The letter came back from Colt Firearms. The pistol was part of a sale where three matching pistols were bought new by a trucking company out west by the name of Marlow Trucking Company, in South Dakota. The gun had never been registered to my dad or anyone other than the trucking company. Marlow Trucking was now out of business; it was another dead end. I became depressed and confused. Why had I been put on this road, again? Why had the gun made its way back to me? The answer would soon come, but not the way I could have imagined.

It is never easy to read a coroner's report about anyone's death, much less, your own father. His height, weight, and eye color were recorded with a gross description of his overall anatomy and build. The cause of death was ruled "brain laceration caused by gunshot." The report told the weight of his brain, the affected areas of the brain, and the affected areas of the brain the bullet had destroyed. It described in detail that parts of my daddy's brain had begun to, or had already died. I couldn't believe that with such damage, he had survived it all; much less talked to us before he finally passed away. It was a gift that was no doubt given to him, and to us, by God. I knew it then as a boy, and it was confirmed again to me now in this report, that my father had absolutely no chance to survive the gunshot wound. Mercy and love from God above kept him here long enough for us to say goodbye.

The call came again from the records department; the copies were now ready. I picked up the folder that was about one inch thick. I took the records down into the basement office area of my house. I began to read the reports… it all began again, and suddenly, I was reliving it all again! Lost, back in time, thirty some odd years ago. The rush of adrenaline, the panic, the fear, and overwhelming sadness came flooding back into my heart. As I read the details, hour by hour, day by day, things were again so familiar to me. Somehow as I read along, I once again felt all the emotions of an eighteen-year-old kid with big dreams, who experienced his whole world, come to a screeching halt. I can't describe the way the medical records took me back, but I could smell the hospital, and I could see and feel my dad. The touch of his hand, the severity of his wounds, and I could feel the 4x4 that I whittled a spud wrench out of as I sat all that time in the waiting room. I could remember the prayers that I prayed, pleading with God to somehow make it all go away and give my dad back to me and my family.

I read for hours, it seemed, and then it began. I got down to the last two days. Daddy's vital signs were all over the board. He was running a fever, no doubt from the infection of his wounds. He was in so much agony, his heart rate and blood pressure were erratic, and he was growing weaker. All the events that happened, all the words that were spoken by doctors and nurses were documented in these records. As I turned and read through the last pages of February 5th, my heart began to pound. It was a very strange sensation, with every sentence, with every vital sign, and my heart began to get heavier, and heavier. It felt like an elephant was standing on my chest. The last hours of my dad's life, I spent at my Aunt Nancy's house, where we were eating Sunday dinner. After we ate, I remember my mom talking to the rest of the family about my Daddy. I walked outside, the air was cold and crisp, the sun was shining, and it was a beautiful winter afternoon. As I waited outside, the same terrible feeling came upon me as the moment my dad got shot. The three times I felt so strongly to pray were the three times my dad's heart had stopped in route to the hospital. I went inside my aunt's house and said that I wanted to hurry and leave. As I stated earlier in this book, we got back to the hospital ten minutes too late, my dad had already passed away. Now, thirty-one years later, because of the gun, I was reliving, no, actually living for the first time, those last 15 minutes. Except now, I was there in his hospital room! As I read the final lines of the report, I heard the doctor's final directives; I sensed the distress in the voices of both physicians and nurses. His vital signs became so much weaker. I agonized over each line, and I didn't want to read further, but, yet I couldn't stop. It seemed with each line, I had to take a deep breath, because I knew what was coming, but, yet I needed so much to remain there and be with my dad.

Suddenly, my father went into cardiac arrest. The doctors were trying CPR, they ordered the defibrillator, they counted down the seconds to shock him, again, and again. In my mind, as I was reading, I was screaming, "Save him! Don't stop trying!" A shot of adrenaline was given to his heart, to no avail. On the last page of the report, the final lines were there, the last moments of the EKG heart tape. I saw the moment the embolism reached his heart. I saw the struggle the Neuro-Intensive-Care unit made to bring him back. His EKG began to fade, as only faint impressions of activity remained.

I couldn't hold back the agonizing moans and tears that came busting out from my soul as the lines went completely flat. My cries came from the deepest center of my soul. The medical report ended with the time of death. I was hurting so bad at that moment I couldn't breathe from the pain and pressure in my chest. I had always worried about the fact that I wasn't with Daddy when he died and left this life of heartache and trouble, but now, this medical report had taken me back to the very day, time, and second. As I cried alone in the basement, I felt as if I were standing by his hospital bed, again. I cannot explain how, and I do not understand the process of what happened to me next. At that moment, I relived and experienced my dad's death. But as the grief and tears became so difficult at the moment he died, I felt the weight of the medical report fall to the table. Then suddenly, silently, in a most incredible and miraculous way, I could feel my dad's love overcome me. It was as if he were standing over me and behind me as I sat in the basement alone. At that moment, in my soul, I heard him say, "Son, it really happened, it is true, I died, but I'm okay. It's okay; I'm still here with you."

I couldn't take it, I lost all my composure, I cried so hard, it had been for what seemed forever since I had felt his spirit. The emotions were so overpowering, I let go of everything that I had bottled up for so very long. After a while, I was exhausted, I was confused by everything that had happened regarding the return of the gun. But, I knew for sure that I had been involved in a most sacred moment between my dad and me. I knew that somehow this blessing was something that only God could provide. Although my dad didn't come back from the grave and appear to me in the flesh, something in my subconscious, the details in the medical reports, the return of the gun, had put me in a place where the heart and soul of man cannot be tethered by the laws of this physical life. What I experienced was spiritual, I testify of its truth, I lived it, I was there, and I have all the proof. It was real, and I thank God for the experience.

Deliverance

Shortly after the events surrounding "the gun," I went to bed earlier than usual. I wasn't feeling well, as my heart had been acting up. That night, I dreamed I was back down at the creek of the Steel Meadow Farm. The place I would always go during my sylvan relaxation attempts, to the most beautiful place on earth. A place where I imagined I could meet the Lord Jesus.

As I stood by the creek in my dream, I saw three Indians riding bareback on horses. They were making their way through the trees coming up the creek toward me. I could tell they were very, very old, in fact, ancient. The horses they rode were ghost white. In my dream I suddenly felt as if they were spirits. In my dream, I looked around the small meadow I stood in, and as I looked, I saw a large eagle feather lying on the ground. I had a feeling that the eagle feather represented the priesthood, and my faith in Jesus Christ. I picked the feather up off the ground and held it with both hands close to my chest, as the three ancient Indian ghost riders made their way up to me. The moment they arrived only one spoke to me. His hair was long and a mix of grey and white. The age in his face and the sound of his voice made me aware that he was indeed a spirit, or an angel of sorts. He had a beautiful, ornate dream catcher and a medicine bag on his side. I began to fear it was the "angel of death." This fear made me hold fast to the eagle feather I held. The old Indian looked at the feather in my hand and he looked at me as if he was looking into my very soul. He said, "What is your name?" I said, "My name is Steve Mathis." He sat on his horse, looking at my feather, "Go in peace, Steve that says Mathis!" He slowly turned his horse and went up the creek with his two companions.

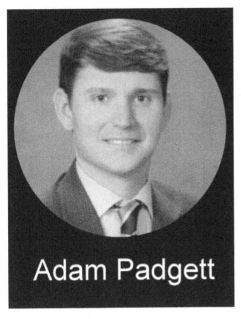

Adam Padgett

Needless to say, I awoke from that dream completely freaked out! It was so intense, and it seemed so very real. I hoped it was a sign that I would get better. In the days that followed, I once again entered into a contract to sell American Fast Print. A young realtor by the name of Adam Padgett, with the Llyon's Group, had really worked hard to get yet another contract. He became a good friend of mine as well. At the same moment, I had yet another heart episode. I saw an ER doctor by the name of Dr. Braun. He told me in the ER that he felt that I was an excellent candidate for cardiac ablation surgery, and it was the first time I had ever heard of it. He gave me a referral and I went to see Dr. Berry. He was a local cardiologist and he too, thought I was a good candidate for this type of surgery. Ablation surgery is when they go into your heart and cauterize nerves around pulmonary veins in your heart. After much thought and prayer, I elected to give it a chance, as opposed to taking medicine and blood thinner for the rest of my life. I was afraid of heart surgery, but I felt like I would have to have faith and make an attempt to get better.

Two days before my heart surgery, the American Fast Print property, Viking Warehouses, finally sold! The wire transfer from the Philadelphia based firm was for 1.1 million dollars! My day of deliverance had come like any other ordinary day, but on this day, it happened, it really happened; my deliverance had come. I was greatly overjoyed. My mind and heart were flooded with so many memories; I knew my life had suddenly changed. And by the way, my heart surgery was a success, and the doctor said all four pulmonary veins needed ablation, and that I would be okay.

Steel Meadow Farm
August 11, 2015

Nowadays I frequently visit with Joey. We mostly talk about the days when we were young. RJ says he has officially "retired" again. I see him from time to time. Jesse is still going strong; he is working a lot now for School District 3 of Spartanburg. Larry Wigington is selling Heart Pine flooring and he loves to talk about the old days, too. Adam Padgett is still young and working hard to lease space for me at the Health-Tex / Viking Development property. Duane Glass is now my only employee; he still picks up the steel containers from the Department of Transportation, and our few remaining accounts. And yes, Dexter Cleveland is still part of my life and a close friend. We meet for lunch to discuss the present issues of the day, but often reflect on all those wild, crazy times, we all shared. I still occasionally talk with Billy Tobias as we have remained friends to this day. He appears to be happy and enjoying life. And as for me, well, let's just say I just had a bumper crop of "jubilee watermelons," the exact same kind that grandpa grew.

I am content now to spend all my days at "the barn" on Steel Meadow Farm. Angela entertains me in my farming. She loves the cucumbers and the fresh vegetables. My children are all grown-up and some moved off. My life is blessed and beautiful. As I write these final lines to the story of the Steel Meadow Farm, the golden finches, hummingbirds, and butterflies feast upon the sunflowers in the front of the barn. The honeybees love the sunflowers, and are obliged to pollinate my vegetables, corn, cantaloupes, and watermelon fields. The Blue Ridge

Mountains still appear in the backdrop of the western sky, as the sun shines upon my little piece of heaven.

In my mind, I still hear the cranes, construction equipment, and the welding machines of my yesterdays. I see the faces of all the people who have helped me along my incredible journey. I can hear the rhythmic clanging of my spud wrenches as I walked the iron, high above the ground, in my youth.

The crickets sing their evening song; the crows scream each morning as they wait to see when I will appear. As the seasons come, and the seasons go, whether in green grass or winter snow, I am at home! It is so ironic to me, as I plant my watermelons and work these fields, that this is the place I wanted so much to leave as a young man, and my home I was forced to vacate for twenty years. A place I longed for, a place I dreamed of and a place I was returned to by the hand of a loving and merciful God.

It seems that fate forced me to live the life of my dad. Mercy and love from the Almighty has given me the privilege to live the life my grandpa experienced, and his dad, and his dad! Yes! Oh yes, life at the family farm. It seems so surreal; I hope I never leave it again. I want so much to be buried here with my memories, my past, my pain, my joy, and my hope. For all my friends and family who have died before me, it is here that I feel them; it is here I remember them. It is still just as breathtaking; it is still just as simple, it is still just as hard as it was when I was a child. If you ever pass by the little town of Cowpens, South Carolina, you should see Steel Meadow Farm place located at 4813 Cannons Campground Road. It is a place time forgot; a gorgeous little farm where the pine trees and fescue blow in the breeze. The fall leaves manifest a brilliant country farm picture against the magnificent evening sky.

I don't know how many more seasons I will be blessed to see and experience this, but I do know that I will cherish them all. With each New Year, the watermelons will grow, the silver queen corn, squash, and okra will be a blessing to me and all those around me. I have discovered the awesome blessing of donating my crops to Mobile Meals in Spartanburg, South Carolina.

Michelin

Andrews Building

Spinning Frame Removal/Adams Plant   **Bowater's Smoke Stacks**

Cherokee Indian Hospital   **1976 Crane**

Steel Meadow Farm

This book is to certify a story, too unbelievable to be true. It is just a small effort and attempt to thank God, and all those lives He put in my path, who helped me get back to where I am today, and to where I want to forevermore remain; back to the *Steel Meadow Farm*!

Thank you for taking this walk back through time with me.

Is this the end? Will I have more to say?

Only time will tell.

Until then, I wish you all the very best.

Leave a legacy,

Stephen Craig Mathis

Dictation ends.
May 23, 2017 5:00 pm

Made in the USA
Columbia, SC
17 August 2021